The
MISANTHROPE's
Guide to Life

{Go Away!}

MEGHAN ROWLAND AND CHRIS TURNER-NEAL

A**adams**media
Avon, Massachusetts

Published by
Adams Media, a division of F+W Media, Inc.
57 Littlefield Street, Avon, MA 02322. U.S.A.
www.adamsmedia.com

ISBN 10: 1-4405-2508-0
ISBN 13: 978-1-4405-2508-7
eISBN 10: 1-4405-2777-6
eISBN 13: 978-1-4405-2777-7

Printed in the United States of America.

10   9   8   7   6   5   4   3   2   1

Library of Congress Cataloging-in-Publication Data
is available from the publisher.

This book is available at quantity discounts for bulk purchases.
For information, please call 1-800-289-0963.

This book is dedicated to the readers of 2birds1blog, who exemplify every day what it means to be a true friend—supportive, caring, and separated from us by a pane of glass.

Acknowledgments

For curmudgeons, we had a surprising amount of support during the writing of our book. The authors would like to thank their parents, Richard Rowland, Diane Rowland, Cameron Neal, and Kay Turner for being incredibly supportive. Thank you to Becca and Geoff Grubbs for providing Meghan with a place to stay and an occasional nutritious meal, and Andie King for her continued love and support. Thank you to our friends, who have been very patient with our nocturnal lifestyles and occasional shouts of "Go away, dammit! I'm writing!" Thank you to Caitlin Pratt for introducing the authors to one another; forgive her, she knew not what she did. Thank you to Grandmother, Mr. von Rosenberg, and the Camel for being exceptions to the "everybody sucks" rule. Our sincerest thanks to everyone at Adams Media who worked on this project—especially Matt Glazer, who was gentle with us since it was our first time (it didn't hurt at all), and Wendy Simard, who cut the suicide jokes but otherwise let our voices shine through. Finally, as always, our deepest thanks to the luminous Jessica Walter. You are the wind beneath our wings.

CONTENTS

Misanthrope *(noun)*:

1. One who hates mankind; a curmudgeon; a loner.
2. The guy in your office who responded to your e-mail of baby photos with, "D–. Passing, but not college material."
3. A realist.

INTRODUCTION

{Like Meeting New People? Neither Do We}

Once upon a time in a small town in Texas, there was a little boy with hair as ginger as the effervescent ale of which his mother did not approve, who did not fit in. One thousand miles away in a suburb of our nation's capitol, there was a little girl whose peg was equally square. While their peers were playing Kick the Can and Seven Minutes in Heaven, they were watching *Murder, She Wrote* and rooting for the killer (played this week by Jessica Walter). As the little boy and little girl got older, not a whole lot changed. Middle school brought with it a lot of therapy, which probably would have been more useful had our heroes not started every session with, "Why don't *you* go first." In high school they finally got their driver licenses, giving them the freedom to skip class and take a "Privacy Power Hour" parked behind the Walgreen's listening to Garbage and smoking stolen menthols.

It was in college when the boy and girl, now not so little, finally met. The boy's dorm was having a "getting to know you" shirts versus skins ultimate Frisbee game, while the girl's dorm held a mocktails and date-rape awareness happy hour. Desperate to avoid participating, both slipped into the campus drug store, eager to buy some vomit-inducing syrup of ipecac. As if guided by a wise-ass guardian angel, their hands simultaneously closed around the same bottle. Startled and annoyed, they locked eyes among the Pop-Tarts and Tampax.

"You look like a nice girl, but I'm facing shirts versus skins here," the boy said.

"I'll see your pasty torso and raise you, '*add a splash of seltzer for a kick!*'" the girl replied.

"Halvsies?"

"Done."

That night as they retched into their souvenir Freshman Orientation '98 cups, each got a glimpse of the moon and felt for the first time it was shining down on someone who could understand them.

The next day as classes began, they both found themselves in Race, Class, Gender: Examining Otherness. As the professor outlined the class, a girl in a torn Bikini Kill T-shirt and hemp cargo shorts raised a trembling hand, weak from a diet of soy and outrage.

"Um, excuse me, sir or madam, if we're problematizing gender, shouldn't we acknowledge the rich tradition of *Her*story?"

"Ugh, *earnestness*," our heroes muttered under their breath in unison. As they heard the echo, the same thought darted through each of their minds: "I'm *not* alone." They looked up, hesitantly turned, and were shocked to recognize each other from the night before. After class was dismissed, the boy took the girl aside, stared intently into her dark, brown eyes and said, "You got hives at Day Care too, didn't you?"

"*Plinko!*" The girl responded. That night, amid a sea of empty Bartles & Jaymes bottles and stubbed-out Marlboro Reds, the two swapped stories about hiding in "privacy bushes" at summer camp, field trip–related panic attacks, and years of spending recess with the nurse, listening to the latest details of her messy divorce. Feeling more and more like they were in the presence of a like-minded equal, they held each other, gently rocked, and cast their eyes toward the heavens. As tears rolled down their cheeks, they cried, "*Who are we?! Who made us?!*" like two confused, just-mutated superheroes, hot off the uranium presses.

Fueled by their Blue Hawaiian liquid courage, they sat down at the computer and started doing research, desperate for a better explanation than a nasty case of the Fuck Yous. After a failed string of dud searches—"go away"; "don't touch me"; "people suck"; "no I don't want to come to your quinceañera"—they stumbled upon an intriguing and provocative term: Misanthrope.

"Misanthrope." "*MIS*-anthrope." "Mis-*ANTHROPE.*" They repeated the word over and over again, exploring the unfamiliar sound and letting it all just wash over them.

The next day they went out and made T-shirts. Several years later they wrote a book, so that Misanthropes everywhere would know how to cope with their natural enemy: *people.*

People are *everywhere.* Even if you've taken to squatting in an abandoned Cold War–era bomb shelter, you'll still have to leave from time to time to pick up some fresh rat traps and Mountain Dew. We've gathered together a quick primer in Misanthrope history, a couple of quizzes so you can determine if you're really a Misanthrope or just a-raggin', and 101 common interaction scenarios with multiple solutions for each. With this book in hand, you should have no trouble reducing your social circle to a single dot.

Great Moments in Misanthrope History

Adam and Eve may have gotten along fine, but Cain beat Abel with a rock for being a show-off. You're not the first Misanthrope in history; as long as there have been groups, there have been people avoiding them. So that you can appreciate our proud and ancient traditions, we present you with a brief misanthro-centric view of history:

- **Ca. 60,000 years ago:** The first aborigines arrive in Australia, finding deserts and the world's most poisonous animals—a small price to pay for dozens of millennia of privacy.
- **220–206 B.C.:** The Qin Emperor builds the Great Wall of China to avoid having to wave at the neighbors.
- **2nd century A.D.:** Early Christians establish the first monastic communities, giving spiritually minded Misanthropes an excuse to hide in the desert.
- **Ca. 1000:** The Maori arrive in New Zealand, the last major land-mass to be settled by man. There is now nowhere left to hide except Antarctica.
- **1347–1353:** The Black Death kills millions in Europe. Survivors revel in free clothes and their own rooms.
- **1492:** Spaniards arrive in the New World and won't leave, no matter how many times the natives yawn and mention having to go to work in the morning.
- **1666:** Moliere's *The Misanthrope* opens in Paris. World in shock by apparent collaboration between Misanthropes and Theater People.
- **1790:** First solitary confinement in the United States at the Walnut Street Jail in Philadelphia. Prisoners dare to dream.
- **1815:** Napoleon is exiled to the remote South Atlantic island of St. Helena and is *very* ungrateful.
- **1820:** Fabian Gottlieb Benjamin von Bellingshausen discovers Antarctica. There is now nowhere left to hide except the moon.

- **1840s:** Manifest Destiny begins when pioneers take covered wagons "to the corner to buy some smokes" and never come back.
- **1848:** Karl Marx develops communism, which combines the inconveniences of central control with the discomforts of sharing and cooperation. Misanthropes worldwide develop nosebleeds without knowing why.
- **1861:** Eleven southern states "wish they could stay for dinner, but will probably just grab something on the road."
- **1867:** The Treaty of London forces Luxembourg to dismantle the defensive walls around the city, despite the Luxembourgers' objections that then people would think they could just show up whenever.
- **1876:** Alexander Graham Bell invents the telephone, then begins calling people "just to talk."
- **1914:** The Panama Canal is completed, drastically shortening shipping times and quashing Jose Padilla y Vega of Cuba's argument that he'd "totally go" to his cousin's wedding in Valparaiso if it weren't for that pesky loop around Cape Horn.
- **1969:** *Apollo* 11 lands on the moon. Goddammit.
- **1986:** 5.5 million people participate in "Hands Across America," joining hands in a massive human chain for fifteen minutes. Seventy-three Misanthropes "just painted their nails, sorry."
- **1993:** Czechoslovakia is peacefully divided into three countries: the Czech Republic, Slovakia, and "Vlad's House—No Trespassing."
- **2010:** Bedbug outbreak in northeastern cities provides urbanites with long-awaited solid reason for not sleeping over.

Quiz #1: **Am I a Misanthrope?** (True/False)

1. I once punched myself in the jaw so I could spend recess in the nurse's office. **T/F**
2. Motivational quotes give me acid reflux. **T/F**
3. Sometimes I pretend to be checking my mail to avoid small talk at the elevators. **T/F**
4. I've waited in line for a *Harry Potter* movie. **T/F**
5. I fucking love Burning Man. **T/F**
6. I don't just attend team-building exercises—I plan them! **T/F**
7. I've prepaid a divorce, just in case. **T/F**
8. Sometimes I wake up in the morning with a song in my heart. **T/F**
9. The sloppiness of children's art does not appeal to me. **T/F**
10. A stranger is a friend you haven't met. **T/F**

The Results

Give yourself one point for answering true on number(s): 1; 2; 3; 7; 9, and give yourself one point for answering false on number(s): 4; 5; 6; 8; 10.

If you got 0–3 points:

Congratulations, I guess. You probably had a lot of fun in student government. You are the belle of every ice cream social. You are probably not a Misanthrope and will continue to bubble through life saying things like, "Hiya, fella!" and "I'm a people person!" with a smile as your umbrella; that is, until someone shoots you.

If you got 4–7 points:

You're probably a normal, run-of-the-mill person with some misanthropic tendencies. Company retreats and potluck dinners are probably hard for you, but you can usually get through the day without hiding in a stairwell, waiting for the Xanax to kick in. You may even have a work friend, but you'll probably alienate him somewhere down the line with your extreme political views.

If you got 8–10 points:

Yowzah. You are a Purell-carrying, pistol-packin', crowd-fearing, hug-dodging, no-nonsense Misanthrope. You send a card instead of attending, which caused a problem at your own wedding. We hope you were able to mail-order this book; we know how stressful it can be to go to the mall.

Now that you know for sure that you're a Misanthrope (and not just a-raggin'), in the absence of a "sorting hat," we've prepared a second *bonus round* quiz that will help you discover exactly what kind of Misanthrope you are.

Quiz #2: **What Kind of Misanthrope Am I?**
(Multiple Choice)

1. *A charity canvasser approaches you on the sidewalk and asks for a moment of your time. You:*
   A. Saw them from down the block and swerved widely to avoid them.
   B. Say, "Sorry, just don't care about whales."
   C. Say, "Sorry, I already gave."
   D. Deck 'em.

2. *A moderately attractive stranger offers to buy you a drink in a bar. You:*
   A. Tell him you have to go to the bathroom, but actually leave altogether.
   B. Say, "You *can* buy me a drink, but you *may* not."
   C. Tell him he's a dear for asking, but your large, violence-prone boyfriend is in the bathroom.
   D. Accept the drink, down it and say, "Thanks, slugger!" while you slap him on the shoulder and walk away.

3. *In a crowded subway car on your commute home, you spot a pregnant woman standing. You:*
   A. Bury your nose in a book.
   B. Ignore her; she's pregnant, but I'm tired.
   C. Give her your seat, but my God are you pissed.
   D. Continue to sit with your feet up on the seat across from you; serves her right for making more people.

4. *An hour before your company's Christmas party, you are:*

A. Turning off your cell phone so no one can call and ask where you are.

B. Getting ready to smuggle your friend Jack Daniel's in—in your bloodstream.

C. Making chocolate reindeer so no one can say you didn't try, damnit.

D. Hiring a stripper with more chest than heart to bust in halfway through and deliver a graphic rendition of "Santa Baby" while you slip out undetected. At that point you will have suffered long enough.

5. *If you feel strong enough, flash back to high school. Your biology teacher tells you to pick partners for a dissection. You:*

A. Bend over and rummage in your book bag until everyone is safely paired off.

B. Snap up the Korean exchange student again because he'll do the work and you don't share a language.

C. Pair off with a jock, stoner, slow kid, or combination of all three. Give them a page to color while you do the work correctly.

D. Pair off with the class vegan, start singing "The Rainbow Connection," and hope she protests her way into a group B+.

6. *Your four-year-old niece asks you where babies come from. You say:*

   A. No one knows.
   B. CVS. You were 30 percent off because you were slightly irregular.
   C. Ask your parent, teacher, community leader, or rabbi.
   D. Romania. And statistics tell us that you'll grow up to be a real troublemaker.

7. *Your neighbor knocks on the door and tells you she's locked out. She asks you if she can stay until the locksmith comes. You:*

   A. Tell her you're so sorry but you were just on your way out, then walk around the block for the next half hour.
   B. Call the police.
   C. Say, "Great, I needed help cleaning the grout! It must be kismet!"
   D. Say no because you just started watching the second season of *Lost*, and that's not a show you can just jump into. We're sure she'll understand.

8. *Your girlfriend tells you that she's pregnant. You:*

   A. Emigrate.
   B. Ask, "Who's the father?"
   C. Marry her and raise the child, but slowly withdraw all of your love.
   D. Find some Romanians to adopt it. Why should the baby trade be one-way?

The Results

If you answered:

Mostly a's:

You are an Avoidant Misanthrope. You are the patron saint of the locked door and turned-off phone. Like a big tit in a strapless bra, if there's a way out, you'll find it.

Mostly b's:

You are a Crotchety Misanthrope. Impatient and sardonic, you keep the world at bay with precision-aimed jets of piss and vinegar. (Mostly metaphorical, but you're not above literal.) While the world may interpret your brash wisecracks as good humor, we know better.

Mostly c's:

You are a Stealth Misanthrope. Heavily socialized, but a people-hater nonetheless, you put the "ass" in passive-aggressive. Always willing to grin and bear it, you appear to be likeable, but may eventually frighten people off with that pulsing vein in your forehead.

Mostly d's:

You are an Asshole. Sometimes it really is that simple.

The Misanthrope's Prayer

Lord, grant me the irritability to deal with those people I cannot avoid, the flight-reflex to avoid those people I can, and the impatience to get it all over with quickly.

Chapter 1

THE AGNEW TO MY NIXON

{ The Misanthrope Among Friends }

Accidents happen. Sometimes Marisa Tomei wins the Oscar, the ESL kid reigns as Homecoming Queen, and a Misanthrope manages to find a friend. While it's nice to finally have someone to put down as an emergency contact (your realtor was tired of getting calls), the opportunity costs of friendship can be a heavy cross for the Misanthrope to bear. For example, did you know that you're expected to see friends on their birthdays *every single year*? Or that they occasionally need to press their bodies against yours in a quick, but meaningful embrace? While that may be enough to send some Misanthropes running for the change of address forms, keep in mind that Linda is a RealDoll and can't bail you out of jail. So we say keep your friends close, but your defense mechanisms closer. Because they know where you live. And they want to play Guitar Hero.

"I'm Not Your Girlfriend, Girlfriend": Handling Fag Hags

Irony is the whip of a sarcastic God. Misers die poor, beauties grow old along with the rest, and homosexual men are surrounded by high-maintenance, chattering women. If a man orders a Sidecar in public, awkward, needy women for miles around will jump up, put on too much makeup, and barrel toward him, baying like hounds on the scent. This is tiring for any gay man, but for the "Misanthrope of an alternate lifestyle" it's a sobbing, hugging, raspberry-flavored purgatory. The gay reputation for endearing bitchiness makes these women almost impossible to dislodge:

Fag Hag: Does this skirt make me look fat?

Misanthrope: Yes! Everything does! You're fat!

Fag Hag: I love our times together.

They're hard to dissuade, but where there's a Misanthrope, there's a way . . .

Man Up

Fag Hags crave male attention without the unglamorous, inconvenient aspect of having a man around. Putting the "dude" back in "gay dude" can sometimes send her screaming into the night. Yell "Fuckin' Seahawks!" and "Touchdown!" at the TV. It doesn't matter if you don't know the rules; she doesn't either. Leave beer cans in a pile on the floor, filed neatly between the "I've been meaning to get to that laundry" pile and the new coffee table you made out of two stacks of pizza boxes. Scratch every part of your body you can find—you'll be amazed at what you can reach. If that doesn't work, start leaving the bathroom door open. It's not pretty, but it works.

The American Dream

Baseball is technically the national pastime, but only because Jimmy Carter refused to sign a bill designating "Laughing at the Less Fortunate" our new top jam. Use this: Instead of getting rid of

The Hags altogether, find a way to make a little scratch off them. Start a paysite called mascaratracks.com, offering footage from a number of hidden webcams, transcripts of 3 A.M. phone calls, and a "fantasy fag hag league" in which players choose a dream team and earn points for every time one of their hags experiences a weight fluctuation, cries so hard she throws up, has a "four mojito meltdown," or goes through any of a number of embarrassing experiences.

Friday Nights with The Fag Hag: A DVD Collection:

- *Beaches*
- *Spice World*
- *Trick*
- *Sex and the City 2*
- *A League of Their Own*
- *Maid in Manhattan*
- *Boys on the Side*
- *The Beautician and the Beast*
- *The First Wives Club*
- *Beaches* (Widescreen)

Ending a Party; or, Don't Let the Door Hit You in the Ass on the Way Out

Occasionally, a brave or foolish Misanthrope will throw a party. You'll need several damage control tactics if you have buyer's remorse: Send out invitations with a clearly stated end time, supply confusing, inaccurate directions, or pay a good caterer to host the party while you spend the evening away. Even with these precautions in play, the Misanthrope can get stuck with guests who just won't leave. Worse, guests keep sighing and saying "We should do this more often . . ."

Bedtime for Bonzo

Just start getting ready for bed. Floss your teeth, wash your face, put on pajamas with a yawning teddy bear on them. Most people will get the hint as early as the flossing, but keep going if your guests prove harder to dislodge. You shouldn't hesitate to don your sleep mask, put soothing ocean sounds on the stereo, climb in bed and get fetal. If this doesn't work, just go to sleep. Maybe they'll be gone in the morning.

It's My Party and I'll Bang Who I Want To

Haul out a basket and announce, "It's time. Keys." No matter how curious some of your guests may be to live it up and just go with it, they won't have time to get up the nerve to say, "Well, I have always wondered . . ." before a more prudish partygoer says, "Disgusting!" or "Not with these fatties, are you kidding me?" Accuse the objector of being a "Prudence Primrose" who has "ruined a perfectly good key party for everyone," and hope the resulting awkwardness sends everyone for their coats.

Portland's Pride

Just slowly but surely cook up a batch of good, old-fashioned crystal meth. Put on your "Kiss the Cook" apron and chef's hat and continue with casual conversation as you lay the drain cleaner, cough syrup, and old batteries out on the coffee table. Distribute goggles and advise your guests to put them on, as "things got kind of *kaboom-y* last time!" As you light up the Bunsen burner, mention that your trademark is to add a little pinch of cilantro for flavor. "It's subtle, but it really brings it all together quite nicely." If your guests have any sense, they'll hightail it for the door. If not, maybe they'll smuggle the meth into Canada for you.

Conversation Topics to Clear a Room:

- Ethnic cleansing
- Restless Leg Syndrome
- John Kerry
- The polyamorous lifestyle
- "Does this look infected?"
- This chick you know who's a Suicide Girl
- That one uncle . . .

Misanthrope as Wingman

Apparently, friends are supposed to "help" one another. Not just in simple, manageable ways like cracking a tough section of a word search or answering the phone with "Turner-Neal Investment Group" because they've used you as a phony reference, but in tangible, inconvenient ways. This can lead to misunderstandings.

Friend: Hey, can you help me?

Misanthrope: . . . yes? Yes. Final answer.

Friend: It's been a long time since I've been with a girl, and I thought you could . . .

Misanthrope: Oh, I'm not sure that's wise. You'd probably want to cuddle afterward and I'd have trouble respecting you after that.

Friend: What? No! I just want you to come out to the bar tonight and be my wingman.

Misanthrope: Wing . . . man?

Friend: Yeah, just try to make the women think I'm cool.

Misanthrope: Isn't that Amstel Light's job?

Lay It on the Line

Misanthropes are envied two things: our clear, ageless complexions, gained by a life spent indoors shunning team sports, and our "charming" bluntness. Save time and cut bullshit by treating the wingman's role like what it is: a sales position. "Listen, Renata, you seem like a sharp girl. I'm gonna level with you. My friend thinks you're hot. I know his septum piercing is a little inflamed right now, but he's clean, in good shape relative to the other people in this bar, and he's hung like a '78 Chevelle. You might do better tonight, you might not, but I can send you home with this perfectly acceptable guy now and save us all a lot of time and trouble." This approach takes all of three minutes, so you have ample time to try again if it turns out you were "too real."

Villain of the Piece

Wait until the lady's attention is diverted, then put on a little show. "Hey!" your friend shouts, "What did you put in her drink?" At this point your friend will take you in a pre-choreographed headlock, and throw you out the door. Upon his return, Sir Galahad will have the perfect opportunity to buy her a drink "to show her not all guys are jerks." Meanwhile, you're outside, free to toddle home and do your drinking in the bathtub, as you prefer.

Gordon Gekko and Warren Buffett walk into a bar . . .

Dress your friend up in the top hat, monocle, and cane from last year's Mr. Peanut Halloween costume, and loudly discuss pork bellies and rice futures, as you slap him on the back and chortle, "you *cad!*" Women are drawn to money like ants to sugar, sharks to blood, and Japanese businessmen to used sports bras.

Obscure Japanese Fetishes:

- Dinosaurs
- Hidden camera footage of women filing their nails while bored at work
- Adult origami
- Unwrapped Christmas presents
- Heimlich maneuver lesbians
- Badminton divorcees
- Pregnant teen hiccups

No Hit Wonder: It Turns Out Your Friend's Band Is Bad

Misanthropes are never in bands, for fear the band will hit it big and they'll have to spend a year on a tour bus with stoned roadies who want to talk about "living the music." For us, the question is not, "Why do rock stars commit suicide?" but "How do they last as long as they do?" Amazingly, nearly every person who is not a Misanthrope is in a band, has been in a band, is looking for a new band, is putting together a band, or just got kicked out of their last band. If you've decided to have a friend, you'll have to go see his band sometime. You'd never ordinarily choose to listen to a death metal tribute to Lesley Gore. You'd never ordinarily conceive of such a thing, but here you are, 10 feet from a man named Bone-splitter, who's clad only in leather and spikes and belting out light '60s pop with a bride-of-Satan twist. After the show, your friend, glistening with sweat and enthusiasm, bounds up to you and hits you with the most passive-aggressive question possible: "So, what did you honestly think?" A Misanthrope is generally incapable of spitting out a tactful lie like a normal person, but we're not without resources.

The Groupie Misdirect

Fuck him in the bathroom right that minute. Like most human endeavors, being in a band is a tail-getting strategy first, foremost, and often exclusively. If you lead him to believe it's working, he won't press for details, and you won't have to use music-magazine broken English like "hot, nasty chords" and "fat beats."

Liquor Is Quicker

You know what a drunk person can't process? "Damning with faint praise." Insist on buying your friend a shot before you talk about the show, and repeat as needed. Shot. "It was interesting." Shot. "I've never seen anything quite like it." Shot. "Bonesplitter is very tall." Shot. By the time you get to "It's the dumbest fucking thing I've ever seen in my life, and if I were a better friend I'd kill you now to save you the shame of living with this memory," he should only be able to say, "Wooo! Rock 'n' roll!"

Deafened by the Awesomitude

"What did I honestly *drink*? Oh, just a few Chardonnays. What? Did I *bike* to the show? No, I took a cab. What? Do I think your band is *hood*? No, you're five white boys from Dutchess County. You'll never be hood."

Set list For the Death Metal Tribute to Lesley Gore:
- "Judy's Turn to Cry (Because She's Being Eaten by Hell-Wolves)"
- "It's My Party (And You'll Die if I Say So)"
- "You Don't Own Me, But I Own the Skulls of All Foolish Enough to Oppose Me"
- "Sunshine, Lollipops, Rainbows, Plague, Madness, and Suicide"

I'll Pay for You to Elope: The Misanthrope in a Wedding Party

From a young age, we're taught to think that friends should share everything—toys, candy, clothes, homework, *Boys!*—what's yours is mine, and vice versa. But what about friends who want to share experiences? Doesn't that seem a little . . . gauche? There's something about the concept of sharing an experience that implies vomiting in a teepee somewhere in Arizona while chasing spirit animals into a world of yesterland and *endless tomorrow*. Fortunately, unless it's 1968 or you went to Skidmore, odds are the most intense experience you'll be asked to share with a friend is to "do them the honor" of being in their wedding party. Unfortunately, that still brings to mind a fair amount of vomiting. Agreeing to be in a friend's wedding party automatically RSVPs you to a world of social functions, all attended by the same boring friends-of-friends, obscure relatives, and one old man of mysterious origin who thinks he's at a bar mitzvah. Worst of all, everyone's gotten wise to your tricks by now—they're all still smarting from the time you scalped your Hole tickets and they had to sit next to a guy named Gideon, who really "felt it." Face facts: Your presence is mandatory. Thank God your enthusiasm isn't.

Misanthropic Groomsman, in the Stairwell, with the *Cat Fancy*

In the animal kingdom, hiding isn't an act of cowardice: It's simple survival. You're no better than a meerkat. Volunteer to take coats, keep an eye on the thermostat, be the only one who knows where the extra bags of ice are—anything that will explain extended absences from the party. You're not hiding in the garage reading *The Poisonwood Bible* with a lap full of cocktail shrimp; you're being helpful!

Studio 54 It

Spend the entire party starting new conversations and excusing yourself to go to the bathroom when you become bored. People might think you have a raging cocaine problem, sure, but the bride and groom will be touched that you invested in social drugs to make their party a hit, and will reward you in the end with a moderately priced, impersonal gift. Win/Win!

Grandpa's Old Forced Interaction Tonic

Hey, what works, works. This is a guide to life for Misanthropes, not a morality play. Drink up.

Excuses to Step Away for a Moment:

- "Gotta purge!"
- "I hear my car alarm"
- Prayer
- "I think I see someone wearing real leather"
- "I got the scoots like you wouldn't believe"
- Eager to use the bidet again
- "Gotta check The Score"
- "I need to touch up my face"

Witty Witty Bang Bang: How to End a Conversation with "That Guy"

There are certain realities in life that a Misanthrope just has to come to terms with. Case in point: That Guy in camo shorts and a Guster shirt will trap you into a conversation about proper lifting technique and how Vince Vaughn is "the man." It doesn't matter the company you keep or how refined you think you are—he's at *every* party. You could be in a Rive Gauche atelier doing shots of absinthe out of Anais Nin's cleavage and That Guy would be there asking Josephine Baker if she'd ever been with a white guy before. Not only is That Guy everywhere, but he's convinced that you, yes you, would love to hear about the time he covered the Democratic National Convention for *The Emory Wheel* and got "respect knuckles" from Dennis Kucinich. ("He was really down to earth. Just a *regular* guy, you know?") Unless you want to stand there all night while he explains what his kanji tattoo means (to him), use one of these escape routes.

Gwyneth Him

Humor him in polite conversation, but speak with a confusingly subtle British accent and pepper in a few transatlantic usages here and there: "I was just mad about the idea of having a happy Christmas, but I fell on my bum in the lift and wound up with a 4-centimeter cut on my leg! Big Ben!" Not even That Guy can handle an "*I'm so delightfully foreign!*" act for that long.

Deflect and Dodge

"It's so funny you should bring it up! You know Caitlin—that girl in the prom dress in the kitchen—she has *super* strong emotions about Alaskan Secession too! Go talk to her about it; she'd love that!" And then immediately hurl yourself through the nearest plate glass window. Remember to tuck and roll though, because you *will* need to run.

Tell Him You Just Found Out What a Cincinnati Bowtie Is

That Guy is the kind of guy who wears a thumb ring, thinks Dane Cook is a badass, and uses Dave Matthews's *Satellite* as foreplay. It's amazing how fast his face will go sheet white when you use "screw" and "trach tube" in the same sentence.

WHAT THAT GUY'S TATTOO MEANS

"Oh this? This is the kanji character for 'light'. I don't know if you know, but kanji is a type of Japanese writing system. To me light symbolizes like, how there's always light at the end of the tunnel and I chose to do it in kanji for my deep respect for Asian culture. It got pretty infected, but no pain, no gain, you know?"

The Morning After: How to Make Up for How Drunk You Had to Get to Socialize the Night Before

Pro: You stayed at your sister's birthday party for four hours last night; a personal best!

Con: You also discussed your porn preferences with her new co-worker.

Con: And justified a racially insensitive joke as being okay because you were "really into community service" in high school.

Con: And ignored everyone's shouts that that stripper pole is actually load-bearing.

Con: And unsuccessfully instigated a heart-to-heart with her friend you've always had a crush on about whether God is a material being or not.

Con: And admitted to an uncomfortably large group that you tried to kill yourself twice in college: once to get attention and once "for realzies."

Con: And partially vomited in a recycling bin, after which you loudly proclaimed, "Return from whence you came, beast!" with a trilled R.

. . . It happens to the best of us. But hey, at least you didn't spend another Friday night at Kinko's making copies of your petition against music on website homepages, right?

The Karen Carpenter

There are a lot of excuses you could give for why you were so out of control last night, but only one will get you sympathy across the board: You mixed alcohol on an empty stomach. Everyone's been there and it was traumatic for them all. It's a cruel part of the Human Experience, like falling in love and getting your heart broken. Except at least a broken heart doesn't make you try to vomit Jägermeister and Chardonnay out of a closed window and ruin a perfectly good denim jacket. Well, normally.

The "I Know You Are, but What Am I?"

If middle school taught us anything, it's that when in doubt, go with a defense mechanism. When your friends inevitably bring up how inappropriately drunk you were the night before, bring up a time they were even more inappropriately drunk and watch them lose themselves in the flashback.

"God, you were a *mess* last night!"

"Yeah I was. Kind of like the time you had six horns of mead at Ren Fest and bought a $600 half-nude mermaid water feature for your studio apartment."

". . . I have to go lay down."

The WASP

Bury it deep down, pretend as if it never happened, and never bring it up with anyone *ever* again. Everyone in Junior League will find out, but since they're WASPs too, they won't talk about it—unless they get drunk.

Other Things You Bought at Ren Fest When You Were Drunk:

- Your kingdom's flag
- Wenches
- $20 on an elephant ride
- A bedazzled codpiece
- A chalice with your crest on it
- Whimsical hair braiding
- Various animal parts
- Five minutes of the King's time

Third Strike: What to Do If Your Friends Want You to Join a Kickball League

Absolutely no part of joining an adult kickball league sounds like a good idea. Its "fun" derives from the perfect storm of physical activity, the outdoors, hand-eye coordination, foot-eye coordination, teamwork, meeting strangers, sweating in front of strangers, mingling, uniforms, public parks, and a giant ball. Didn't we leave this all behind at eighth-grade graduation? What's next, adult rope climbing and scoliosis testing leagues? No, thank you. And yet, with more and more young urban professionals joining adult kickball leagues as a way to meet new people, there's an increasing chance that your friends will want you to be the ninth member of the Phoenix Windcatchers. Here's how to kick *that* idea in the balls.

Make New Friends

But do so in a nonathletic, anticommunity environment, like in the aisles of liquor stores, anger management classes, and grammar blog forums. I mean, you're not a nerd, after all.

Exploit Your Friends' Childhood Insecurities

Unless you're friends with the tiny demographic of Americans who actually enjoyed middle school, your friends were horribly insecure about something (or more probably, many somethings) in their youth. Find out what that was. Use high school friends, parents, siblings, yearbooks, and especially diaries. Scan the pages for shaky handwriting and i's dotted with pentagrams instead of hearts and you'll find what you need:

"Dear Diary,

Jason Corin wouldn't dance with me at his bar mitzvah tonight because he said my hands were too clammy, so I locked myself in the bathroom and ate two helpings of brisket and cried. Michelle eventually talked me out, but then I got winded doing the Cotton-Eyed Joe and vomited all over the gift bag table. *I wish I lived in Paris!!!!*"

Casually suggest she not pitch, for fear the ball slides out of her sweaty hand and costs them the game. *Au revoir,* ball du kick.

Magnum, P.I. Your Way Out of It

Show up to the first practice in a pastel Izod shirt tucked into terry cloth jogging shorts, tube socks, a crisp new pair of Keds, and the icing on the cake—hair. Everywhere. Warm up before practice with some extra-deep lunges and remind your new teammates that these hammies aren't going to warm themselves up. Unless there's a mystery in Oahu that desperately needs solving, they'll send you back to the dugout until you, "take kickball seriously."

Other Things Girls Dot Their I's with During the "Difficult Years":

1. Broken hearts
2. Swastikas
3. Faces with expressions that vary according to their mood
4. Teardrops
5. Nothing, because she's an *individual*
6. The "Om" symbol (during the yoga unit in Gym)

Chapter 2

PLANES, TRAINS, AUTOMOBILES, AND SONS OF BITCHES

{ The Misanthrope in Transit }

It's a deodorant-straining 85 degrees. The air is hot, humid, and heavy with the smell of partially digested kimchi. You're trapped in a small, airless chamber surrounded by three-dozen strangers, all of whom have the fixed soul-less gaze of the damned. (Except for the guy next to you. His lazy eye is rolling around like a Magic 8 Ball furiously shaken by a thirteen-year-old girl trying to break a streak of "Outlook Not So Good.") You're underground. You're tired. You're late. No, this isn't the GitMo Express; this is your everyday commute. Now get your armpit off my croissant.

Leg Room > Dignity

It's easier to find true love than get on an airplane these days. Airlines want all kinds of information—name, weight, ties to known terrorist cells—when all you want to do is get to Sioux Falls, sign the papers, get it all notarized, and take your copies home. With airport screening becoming more and more like a good third date, sometimes it's worth it to take the good old anonymous bus. It's also a great choice for relocating because it gives you a good amount of travel time to get your thoughts in order. With $14 and a duct taped-up trash bag full of Formula 1 T-shirts and broken memories, any just-paroled Judith Light-stalker can see America, one thirty-minute convenience store pit stop at a time. While it's great to get out there and explore your fresh start you need to do some thinking. And you can't do that if you're sitting next to a mustachioed Puerto Rican grandmother anxious to recount the saga of her recent hysterectomy ("—so I said, take it all! If the cat can handle it, so can I!") Next time another passenger looks like they're about to sit next to you and open up, here's how to make them keep walking.

It's Not Ketchup

Gaze fixedly out the window. Right as your potential seatmate is about to sit down, nonchalantly glance over, revealing a moderate amount of blood splattered across your face. Where you get that blood is between you and your god—all that matters is that it's there, and that is in no way weird to you.

Save Me

As soon as the other passenger's fanny hits the seat, turn to them, smile warmly, and say, "Let me ask you something. Do you know where you're spending eternity?" Religion is to small talk as bedwetting is to a sleepover, and they will leave you there in your puddle of metaphysical urine.

I Pine for You

As soon as you notice a fellow passenger eyeing the seat next to yours with hopeful eyes, shift positions so they can see that you already have a seat mate—your ventriloquist's dummy, Woody! Have a heart-to-heart with old Woods about how you felt the noon show went:

Misanthrope: So, Woody, what'd you think of the noon show?

Woody: I don't know Hank. I was a little disappointed. I just felt like my performance was a little *wooden*, you know?

Misanthrope: Oh, Woody! Keep up jokes like that and our partnership will *splinter*!

Woody: Oh, Hank, don't say that! I really think we're *kindling* some good theater here.

Misanthrope: Say Woody, that sure is a pretty lady over there. Oooh, she's coming this way!

Woody: Quiet, ya idiot, let *me* do the talking.

Anyone who sits next to a ventriloquist is the *real* dummy.

ACTRESSES TO STALK AFTER GETTING A RESTRAINING ORDER FROM JUDITH LIGHT:

Alyssa Milano, Katherine Helmond, Annie Potts, Meredith Baxter, and Paula Poundstone

Flying Solo: Practical Tips for the Airborne Misanthrope

If dignity were a slug, then air travel would be an eight-year-old boy with a shaker of iodized salt. It was never "nice" to be in the air with 100 strangers, but at least once upon a time you could carry on creature comforts like box cutters and toothpaste. Nowadays even a bottle of Sun-In is considered potentially hazardous (making it virtually impossible to take off a brunette and land in a Whitesnake video). When you have to be in Jacksonville for the hearing and your travel options are limited to taking a plane, being a "bus person," or Amtrak (the horror!), it's time to face the friendly skies. But let us help you help yourself—here are some tips to make the entire process easier.

Xanax vs. NyQuil

It is so much easier to get through a flight if you're already flying high. Both Xanax and NyQuil will drowse you up beautifully and mellow you out enough to enjoy the in-flight movie, *Ernest Goes Green*.

Don't Have a Book That Will Start a Conversation

It shouldn't have been chosen for you by Oprah, it shouldn't have a pretty illustration on the cover, and it definitely shouldn't be scripture for anyone. Leave *The Secret* at home and bring *Helter Skelter* instead. (Feel free to chuckle and highlight at your discretion.)

It's Less Embarrassing Than Being a Vegetarian . . .

Order a kosher meal. Not only will you get it first, but the existence of actual quality control for your meal will reduce your risk of "air trots." (This statement has not been evaluated by the FDA.)

Carry on Shirley MacLaine's Meditation Tapes

Because that's an actual thing. If only more screen legends of yesteryear would tape themselves talking about chakras in a soothing voice.

Get a Seat in the Back by the John

People who won't even donate to Jerry's Kids shouldn't sit in the emergency exit row. Make sure you take this into account before choosing a seat. There's nothing more uncomfortable than responding to the flight attendant's, "Will you be willing to help in the event of an air evacuation?" with "The Lord helps those who help themselves, girlie." Try to sit in the back near the lavatory; it greatly lessens the chance that you'll fall into someone when you stagger down the aisle during your Quil-ed out trip to the john.

"ERNEST" B-SIDES:

Ernest Checks His Blood Sugar; Ernest Goes to Canada for Inexpensive Prescription Drugs; Ernest Has a Mild Heart Attack and Suddenly Gets All Spiritual; Ernest Can't Find His Glasses Anywhere; Ernest Sits Down at the Kitchen Table, Buries His Head in His Hands, and Weeps

---

Rolling Horrors: Wheeled Backpacks

Question: If someone were driving down a busy highway at 80 miles per hour and suddenly slammed on their brakes to rummage around their trunk hoping to find half of yesterday's Nutragrain bar, would that be considered "acceptable behavior" or "graduate-level dumbfuckery"? Now, extra credit, explain how that's different from stopping your rolling briefcase in the middle of the crowded subway terminal to fish out the Levinson file and make sure it was properly notarized? People with rolling briefcases drive like narcoleptic Chinese grandmothers, except a thousand times worse. Dodging the other bleary-eyed commuters in the morning is hard enough; you shouldn't have to play chicken with a first-day paralegal dragging her rolling briefcase full of reference books and daily affirmations behind her. So you've got back problems? Well, which do you think will be worse for your back: carrying a tote bag like a grown-up or being savagely beaten and left for dead in a stairwell?

To use a rolling briefcase/backpack is to defy all human decency and such people deserve what they get.

The Belle of the Ball

Fine, if they want to take up as much space as humanly possible, so will you. Put on your biggest hoop skirt and longest forearm crutches (because, of course, you have several of each) and zigzag wildly along the platform, stopping occasionally to spin around and admire the dramatic flare of your skirts. They gave you an inch, and you took a mile.

Hazed and Confused

As the subway approaches, grab the rolling backpack and throw it onto the third rail, as your victim's "very important papers" rooster-tail down the tunnel in the train's wake. Turn and shout, "Now chug, *freshman!*"

Where There's a Will, There's a Rickshaw

The next time they pause, sit down on the backpack, slap them on the shoulder and say, "University City, please! Chop-chop!"

Slyly, Oh So Slyly

Unzip the briefcase slightly, pour in your morning latte, and close it again. By the time they get to the office, the churning action of their frantic little steps will have soaked not only their paperwork, but also their copy of *Eat, Pray, Love* and "accidents happen" change of slacks.

> **STROLLER DERBY:**
>
> The only contraption more dangerous than the rolling briefcase is the child-in-a-stroller. Women who are loving, protective mothers above ground use their toddlers as battering rams once below. Nothing speeds up a meandering tourist looking for the F train faster than a swift crack across the Achilles tendons from a full Maclaren. These women are awful, but there's nothing you can do to them short of making a wheelchair-bound friend strap on shin guards and letting the games begin.

Leaving Your Chicken Bones on the Seat Next to You—Handling the Absurd Things People Do on Public Transit

In the past several decades, America's understanding of what a "family" is has undergone significant changes. Children today are not necessarily raised by a mother and father, but may be raised by a single parent, a same-sex couple, or, apparently, roving packs of rabid wolves. Having a mother who eats rabbit brains is the only acceptable excuse for certain dramatic lapses in passenger etiquette. Who else but a feral child would enjoy a platter of peel-and-eat shrimp on the bus or tweeze their chin hairs while waiting for the train? A century ago, the sight of a woman's ankle was taboo; today you're considered a prude if you flinch when your seatmate gives herself a Brazilian between stops and tosses the hairy cloths on the floor. In a world where dignity is now as passé as organized religion and hemp chokers, what's a Misanthrope to do?

Stand There in Mute Horror

You can't unsee this.

Exhibit A

Surreptitiously take a picture. The next time someone asks you how you can hate people, show them your snapshot of Tatianna cream-bleaching her five-o'clock-in-Kiev shadow at the bus stop and say, "The prosecution rests."

Entrepreneurship

Open your own charm school. Because clearly there's a need.

Lie, Cheat, Steal, and Kill

They broke the social contract first.

Move to France

They don't groom themselves at all and you can drink during the day!

Straight-Up Masturbate

Because at this point, why not?

Rattle a Soda Can Full of Nickels at Them

Hell, it works to scare away cats.

Go Live with an Uncontacted Amazonian Tribe

At least they have an excuse.

> ## "CHEAP SOCKS!":
> ## WHEN PEOPLE SELL THINGS ON THE SUBWAY:
>
> As uncomfortable as it is to watch your fellow passengers water-pick their back molars, it doesn't really affect you unless they peg you with an errant jet. Itinerant vendors, however, will come right up to you with a trash bag of loose batteries, irregular men's briefs, nudie pens, glow sticks, bags of Skittles, phone cards, leftover New Year's glasses where you look through the zeros in 2008, and salad tongs and hit you with a pleading "You buy sir?! You buy?!" They move so quickly and so quietly they're almost impossible to avoid, but they usually go away after they've sufficiently scared you. They live on fear, not the profits from novelty necktie sales.

Even Mussolini Did It: The Courtesy Wave

Fact: There are other people in this world—other loud, obnoxious, mouth-breathing, space-occupying people. In order to coexist with these people peacefully (thereby interacting with them as little as humanly possible), it's important to remember to be civil. You don't necessarily have to like your fellow man—you just have to not kill him. The Vehicular Courtesy Wave exemplifies this concept beautifully: A motorist in the lane next to yours needs to merge and properly conveys this by signaling. Being a decent human being, you slow down and give them ample room to merge. To acknowledge this small act of civility, they raise their hand in a brief wave, as if to say, "Hey, you just made my life slightly easier; thanks for that." You then get a warm, tingly sensation all over and return the wave, as if to say, "You know what? I hope you don't choke on steak and die tonight." You two then go your separate ways, never to cross paths again. It's a beautiful, beautiful thing. And yet whereas Misanthropes, the so-called "antisocial" members of society can grasp this concept perfectly, thousands of "normals" disregard it every day. Here's how to correct them.

The Direct Approach

You know what says, "That wasn't very nice?" A rock thrown through the back window with a note wrapped around it that says, "That wasn't very nice."

The "Can We Keep Him??"

Extend your right hand about a foot in front of you. Now, while remaining cool, calm, and collected, extend your middle finger and leave it there. Indefinitely. His destination is now yours. Follow him home. Follow him around the house, middle finger all the while calmly erect. Do some light yard work with him. Catch up on *Sons of Anarchy* with him. Tuck his children into bed with him, make love to his wife with him, and finally, on the eve of his son's fifth birthday, when you and your middle finger have been accepted as an eccentric, yet loveable member of the family, gently break it to them that it's time for the two of you to ride off into the sunset and help another family learn what an asshole their father is. When the child starts to cry and whimper about how you just can't go, hug yourself ever so slightly—you've made your point.

PEOPLE WHO DIDN'T GIVE COURTESY WAVES:

Adolf Hitler, Ted Bundy, Benedict Arnold, George Wallace, the inventor of jean shorts (cleverly named "Jorts"), that dude who ate that chick, Dracula

The Scourge of Society: Metro Pole Leaners

Misanthropes are big believers in situation ethics. Nearly every action can be excusable if performed in the pursuit of privacy, and our definition of "self-defense" is amazingly broad. There is however one act so depraved, so wicked, so inexcusably abominable that not only will no Misanthrope ever perform it, but which compels us to pursue its perpetrator across time and space in order to exact bloody vengeance. We refer, of course, to leaning on the metro pole of a busy car during rush hour. There is no reason to take up the whole pole with your torso while the other passengers scatter and fly like balls in a bingo cage at every stop. If you see someone leaning on the metro pole, it's your duty as an American to stop them.

Joan Collins Justice

Your boss might look at you funny when you show up to the meeting in a conservative Brooks Brothers suit and a giant blood-covered diamond cocktail ring, but it's still worth it. As stylish dressers have always known, a good accessory is one that you can dress up or down . . . or drive into someone's kidney.

Le Jour de Gloire Est Arrivé

Misanthropes seldom rebel in overt ways. Think about it: popular uprising, mass revolt, the voice of the people, and so forth are just not their style. That said, sometimes a surly, violence-craving mob is the surest means to an end. Leap onto the handicapped seat and deliver a ringing oration about how the proud commuters of the blue line will suffer this tyranny no longer. The very tiles cry out for the blood of the oppressors. Will you see your children and grandchildren doomed to a life of staggering desperately at every stop, or will you act to destroy the pole-leaners now and for all time? With any luck, your fellow riders will rise as one to administer some mob justice, and some seats will open up!

The Kindness of Strangers

Find a good, sturdy handhold somewhere on the pole-leaner's person and hang on. Especially recommended parts to grip are a handful of thigh meat, a long curly beard, or a full, ponderous jowl.

APPROPRIATE THINGS TO LEAN ON:

A sturdy wall, a balanced portfolio of prudent investments, a quad cane, a nearby man (when overtaken by the vapors), a close-knit support network of friends and family, Bill Withers

INAPPROPRIATE THINGS TO LEAN ON:

Anything made out of trick wood, a Jenga tower, your grandmother who has an awful time with vertigo, your abusive boyfriend, your absentee lab partner, Eddie Murphy's unerring ability to rise above a flawed script and remind us all why America fell in love with the cinema

"No, I can talk, I'm just on the bus"—Cell Phone Conversations on Public Transportation

Cell phones have, by and large, made Misanthropes' lives tremendously easier. The portability allows you to be on a "very important call" when you run into that kid from freshman year everyone called "The Crow," and the rise of text messaging has made face-to-face verbal interaction virtually obsolete! It's all very exciting. That being said, cell phones can also be incredibly irritating when they fall into the wrong hands. Whereas a Misanthrope wields a cell phone like Sir Arthur and his mighty Excalibur keeping enemies at bay, the common man uses it to actually talk to people. Like, all the time. For funzies, even.

Daddy Issues

Whip out your cell phone, pretend to place a call, and loudly recite the lyrics to Harry Chapin's "Cat's in the Cradle" in conversational cadence. Feel free to trail off into choking sobs and press your hand against the pane of glass, as if your jailhouse daddy were on the other side.

Oooh, How Meta . . .

Tap the person on the shoulder, apologize for interrupting, and explain that there's a marvelous new fad called blogging that allows assholes who want to share their "thoughts" with the world to do so, but in silence. Offer to help her to come up with a catchy URL address and point out that social media is the key to any blog's success, so if you were her, you'd reserve @BusCunt as soon as possible.

Urinate on Their Phone

It's not classy and you might pull a muscle, but it's the trifecta of efficiency: It'll end their conversation, make them think twice before they do it again, and take care of those 20 ounces of Mountain Dew you've been holding since West 4th Street.

RECENT TWEETS FROM @BUSCUNT:

4:34 P.M. Sorry I haven't tweeted for a few minutes, Amber just called

4:36 P.M. @TrainBitch haha lol

4:37 P.M. @TrainBitch brb gotta call my gynecologist and see if she can see me tomorrow, there's an "issue"

4:39 P.M. @TrainBitch no, nothing like that lol (I wish), I got a robo-call from the health department saying I might have been exposed to something and I just want to go in and make sure

4:41 P.M. @TrainBitch well not yet but they say you can have it for a long time without having any symptoms

4:42 P.M. @TrainBitch I should totally blog about this

Move It or Lose It: How to Make Someone Move Their Bag So You Can Sit Down

Man, there's nothing like a faux-leather boho bag with brass hardware from Payless. It worked hard in high school, was captain of both the JV and Varsity field hockey teams, got a community service–based scholarship to a small liberal arts college in upstate New York and got a degree in history with a minor in geography. Now, thanks to the dismal economy and somewhat obvious unrealistic higher ed choices, its stuck in a dead-end sales management job in its uncle's office and just wants to go home, drink half a bottle of Kendall Jackson Chardonnay and watch *Cash Cab* until it falls asleep. *Oh, wait a minute*, that's not a faux-leather boho bag with brass hardware from Payless—that's *me*! A faux-leather boho bag with brass hardware from Payless is primarily made out of pleather and spray paint and inorganic matter doesn't have broken dreams or the ability to feel pain. But thank God the bag's comfortable on that seat. I'll just continue to stand, though, thanks. Don't worry about me.

Make Like The Fonz and Sit on It

And when they point out that you're sitting on their bag, lift up one of your hindquarters, look down, look back at them, calmly say, "So I am," and go back to reading *The Atlantic.*

Hit on It

"I'm sorry, I just, I never do this, but I couldn't help but notice you when I got on the bus. You have the brightest buckles I have ever seen in my entire life and I've been like, hypnotized by them for the past five minutes. But you must get that all the time. Well, I just felt compelled to tell your—or *you*, rather! I'm all tied-tongue—I mean tongue-tied! Ha ha, I'm sorry, I'm just a little flustered." And then extend your pointer finger and run it ever so gently along one of the zippers while softly biting your lower lip. Trust me, she'll move it.

Threat-Level Prada

Find the conductor and report the bag as a suspicious package. They'll probably just ask her to move it, but there's just a chance this will end with her and her purse being interrogated side-by-side in the bowels of the subway by overweight transit police.

> If possible, report the suspicious bag anonymously. If it turns out to be a weapon and you've accidentally foiled a major terrorist operation out of spite, you don't want to have to get a medal from the mayor in a big ceremony.

Chapter 3

IT'S FIVE O'CLOCK SOMEWHERE—DOES THAT MEAN I GET TO GO HOME NOW?

{ At Work with the Misanthrope }

Despite the off-the-charts popularity of the feel-good sitcom *The Office* and the long lines of applicants seeking jobs at any cost, work sucks. Besides the basic concept of "people telling you what to do," work is also a notorious hotbed of small talk and awkward social gatherings. Most Misanthropes are Olympic-level sprinters, solely from bolting to and away from the coffee machine as fast as they can to avoid being invited to a coworker's daughter's junior ballet jamboree. (She's the youngest ladybug they've ever had!) While we're not in the position to provide you with job listings for the Galapagos Islands DMV—they offer dental, so we've already applied—we have gathered some advice for other on-the-job pitfalls.

Marginally Less Drunk than Your High School Guidance Counselor: Choosing a Misanthropy-"Friendly" Profession

Most of the ideal occupations for a Misanthrope don't really count as "professions." Tycoon, heiress, and "off-Broadway producer" are all subdivisions of "idle rich," a nice gig for anyone but especially coveted by Misanthropes—with utility prices climbing, keeping the electric fence on all day requires deep pockets. If you're not lucky enough to have a grandfather with some oil wells or a mother whose $50-a-day scratch-off habit finally paid off, consider one of these vocations.

Writer

This is one of the few jobs that actually requires solitude; not even the snuggliest morning person could write a good paragraph with someone nearby asking him to help reorder a Netflix queue. Writers also fall under the general heading of "creative types," which means that when you scream, "Go away, be quiet, or kill yourself *right now!*" it'll come across as a high-strung writer's temperament and not a pre-rifle-in-a-tower warning sign.

Long-Haul Trucker

Just you, the open road, and the audiobook of *American Psycho*. A Misanthrope can excel as a cargo driver, since another man's loneliness is our contentment. An added perk is that truckers generally only meet lizards, diner waitresses, and other truckers, none of whom are noted for warmth. If they invite you in, it's for a shot of bourbon or a depressing sexual experience, and in either case you'll be expected to leave directly afterwards.

Wilderness Lady

Remember Dian Fossey, the blood-and-thunder gorilla lady to Jane Goodall's sweetness-and-light chimpanzee lady? The only reason Fossey never won a Misanthropy Lifetime Achievement Award is because it's impossible to get enough Misanthropes together to have an awards gala. It's a toss of the coin whether holing up in the jungle with only guns and apes for company will bring you fame as a "committed researcher" or suspicion as "potential Unabomber," but in either case, if journalists come, you can sic the apes on them.

Night Watchman

The concept sells this one: They need someone to be in the office, because no one else is going to be there. If someone shows up, they're not supposed to be there, and you can taze them or bop them with a nightstick, depending on how fast you feel like moving. In the meantime, you can eat Queen Anne cherries and read movie magazines like a '50s starlet. Solitude + potential for violence + candy = one content Misanthrope.

POOR CAREER CHOICES FOR THE MISANTHROPE:

Kindergarten teacher, greeting card poem composer, stripper, United Nations Goodwill Ambassador, marriage therapist, census worker, teen pop sensation, Miss America

SWF Seeks Understanding 401(k) for Long-Term Relationship: The Job Interview

Career counselors love telling you that you should treat any job interview like you're having a conversation with a friend-of-a-friend at a dinner party. That would be helpful advice, if you actually liked going to dinner parties and talked to friends-of-friends about things other than how dry the meat is and those goddamn wrong-number dialers. Unfortunately, as long as we live in a society where money is exchanged for goods and services, every Misanthrope is going to have to endure a job interview at some point in his life. Luckily for you, recruiters and HR managers tend to ask the same series of questions, and those questions generally fall into two categories: questions about your work experience and questions about your personal life. It tends to be the latter question that gets a Misanthrope in trouble. Nothing says "unhirable" like answering the question, "What do you like to do in your free time?" with, "Skeet-shooting and finding plot holes in *Soap*." If management is trying to get an idea of who you really are, here are some dos and don'ts that will trick them into thinking the answer is "normal."

What is your biggest asset?

DON'T: I'm slightly more competent than a dustpan and I swear to God I won't set anything on fire.

DO: I work well independently and coworkers love my quick wit.

What is your biggest weakness?

DON'T: A fresh box of Benadryl and a *Doctor Who* marathon.

DO: Pecan *saaaaaaaaandies*! [Pat stomach.]

Give an example of a time you solved a problem at your last job.

DON'T: An angry client came in to talk to our office about "accountability" once, so I put on an entire tube of lip-plumping lip gloss, faked a nut allergy, and hung out in the ER until the problem just kind of solved itself.

DO: Just one? I didn't know we were remaking *Sophie's Choice* today!

Do you like to travel?

DON'T: Mass transportation isn't really my "thing," per se.

DO: Do I! I backpacked through Europe for an entire summer after college and learned so much about life. I got "Wanderlust '98" tattooed on the small of my back so I never forget how it felt to feel that free, you know? Wanna see it?

What are your hobbies?

DON'T: Taxidermy, finding really obscure scenes from *Labyrinth* on YouTube, napping, and telling telemarketers to "hit the showers."

DO: Cooking, working out, community service, and spending time with my friends and family.

Well, thank you for coming in today. We'll let you know either way as soon as we've made a decision.

DON'T: Well, aren't you a saint.

DO: Shake their hand and smile—at the same time. It'll feel unnatural, but then again, doesn't everything the first time around?

This is My "Work" Bathrobe—How to Become a Remote Employee

As communications technology has developed, many people have found it difficult to maintain the division between their working and personal lives. E-mail, telephones, and rectal tracking chips have made it easier for coworkers and supervisors to contact employees at home, threatening the traditional work-life balance. However, as in so many other situations, the family man's loss is the Misanthrope's gain. With a little luck and some skillful manipulation, the clever Misanthrope can find himself assigned to work from home, "telecommuting" into the office via technology while remaining safely and quietly at home.

Allergic to Work

Begin complaining of vague, yet troublesome symptoms like itching and a scratchy throat, which gradually worsen—if you're committed, a weekend of heavy smoking can add a convincing rasp to your voice, and poison ivy welts look a lot like hives to the untrained and/or squeamish eye. Announce often that you're going to the doctor. After a few weeks, reveal that your doctor has discovered you're allergic to some substance that pervades the office, be it carpet fibers, cleaning products, or the new kid's "sporty" body spray, and you'll have to begin working at home. If your boss balks, sigh and mention the Americans with Disabilities Act. You'll be clocking in from bed in no time.

Munchausen's by Fictional Proxy

If you're like most Misanthropes, you've responded to friendly questions about your family with a grunt or, at best, a mumble. Now, your vagueness will pay off. Weeping, go into your boss's office and tell him about your poor, beloved mother/father/uncle/ aunt who has no one else in the world, and who has been diagnosed with a dread disease. It's best to be vague about the disease to forestall a company fun run to "raise awareness" of it, so just mention that a number of bags and tubes need to be cleaned out regularly and he should be too uncomfortable to pry. You can still work, of course, it's just that you need to be on hand, in case—God forbid!—one of the tubes should clog . . .

The Hail Mary

"Mr. Rheingold, I need to tell you something. I'm a Misanthrope. I would be much more productive if you would let me work from home, where I wouldn't have to answer questions about whether I saw *American Idol* last night." It's a long shot, but sometimes fortune favors the bold.

> "Work is the refuge of people who have nothing better to do."
> —Oscar Wilde

"Miss Rowland, I'm Afraid My Going to Hell Is Not on the Printed Agenda": Meetings Management for Misanthropes

Misanthropes have never been known for agreeing with the majority opinion, but it can happen. For instance, in common with nearly everyone else, we hate staff meetings. Between *People* magazine, Bono, and the United States Congress, most Americans get 500 percent of the RDA of self-important prigs babbling on about nothing, yet the staff meetings continue. Ditching them completely may not be an option, since work pays the rent and homeless shelters are usually communal, but it may be barely possible to get through them with one's dignity intact.

Option A: Virgin Sacrifice

If power corrupts, it might as well corrupt in a useful way. If you're above even one person in your office hierarchy, make her go as your envoy, having trained her to say "Miss Rowland is very busy, but she values these meetings and sent me to attend and report back." Even if you're relatively low-status, there's probably someone you can strong-arm into taking the bullet for you. Berchtold may be new to this country and most of its commonly spoken languages, but he's *so* eager to please . . .

Option DSM-IV: Dissociative Identity Disorder

According to some psychiatric professionals, persons exposed to severe trauma can sometimes have their personalities "split," creating more identities to handle the psychic burden. This is the "multiple personality disorder" dramatized in *The Three Faces of Eve*. The next time you're stuck in an interminable meeting, see if you can spin off a persona that can stand, or even enjoy it: Eleanor, the Attentive Worker who believes that Synergistic Communication Strategies Enable Worker Empowerment Strategies. She may not be the zestiest superego to share a body with, but it might be worth it to have someone else around to attend meetings, wait in line at the DMV, and apologize for you.

Option 23 Black: Run Numbers

You know what's more fun than talking about long-term market placement strategies? Gambling. Prior to each meeting, set up an elaborate betting pool. Which word will be used more: "paradigm," "synergy," or "proactive?" How many PowerPoint presentations will there be, how many slides will they have, and which will feature the most clip art? Try to avoid subjective categories like "who was the biggest kiss-ass?"—those deliberations could go on all night.

Meeting Topics:

- Choosing a Time for a Subsequent Meeting
- Deciding Which Meetings are Productive

- We're Not Leaving Until Whoever Ate All the Snickerdoodles Comes Forward, I Can Sit Here All Day
- Should Our New Logo Be Navy Blue or Cadet Blue?
- I Realize This Isn't Work-Related but I Need Advice About My Marriage
- Did Anyone Catch *Glee* Last Night?

Three Days of Hell, but We Get Free Pens: Surviving a Conference

According to behavioral psychologists Thomas Holmes and Richard Rahe, the three most stressful events a person can endure in their lifetime are the death of a spouse or child, divorce, and attending a work conference. Well, technically the third is marital separation, but from where I'm standing, more refrigerator space and less morning sex seems significantly better than spending five days straight with your coworkers in a Daytona Marriott. Conferences take all of the glorious moments of solitude peppered throughout your workday and turn them into a group activity. Commuting, bathroom breaks, meals, downtime—none of these are your own anymore. They're for you and your coworkers to *share*. Assuming you've done your best and failed to get out of going to the conference altogether, here are some ways to minimize the awkward forced interaction.

The Old Trusty: "Something Must Be Going Around . . ."

Something is always going around. Even when something isn't going around, it's still going around. And you've caught it. Where'd you catch it? It's always a good idea to get a kid in the mix. Kids are always catching newfangled illnesses that people born before 1980 can't handle gracefully. If you don't have a kid of your own, just say you were babysitting for a friend or loved one. If that seems too far-fetched, get really smug about how we live in such a take, take, take society, so you decided to do something about it and joined your local chapter of Big Brothers Big Sisters. If people are still asking questions, nothing shuts down a conversation with the common man faster than dropping a hard C.O.: court-ordered community service with a disadvantaged group "to gain sympathy." Then all you have to do is sit back and enjoy spending a few hours a day at the conference and the rest of the time being a "trooper" in your hotel room, six mini Cuervos and an episode of *Rick Steves' Europe* deep.

Keep It in the Family: The Cousin Conundrum

It's always a good idea to have a "cousin" in every city. And that cousin should always be younger, a junior in college, freshly out of a relationship, and still undeclared. That way when your office goes out for a team dinner, you can pull the old, "Oh, I wish I could join you, but my cousin goes to [insert college in close proximity to location of conference] and is having a really hard time this year. My aunt would kill me if she knew I was this close and didn't stop by." Not only will this get you out of an awkward corporate dinner, you can also feel free to spend all day on your phone "coordinating" with your cousin about your plans for later that night. If the economy has forced you to share a hotel room with one of your coworkers and you have to go somewhere, there are more than 700 Olive Gardens in this country—get out there and find your America.

Meet Your New Best Friends: Laptop, Furrowed Brow, and Forceful Typing

When in doubt, sit with your back facing the wall and/or a window (if possible), open a blank Excel spreadsheet, and forcefully enter numbers at random with a furrowed brow and concerned look on your face. If anyone saunters over with a corn muffin and the God's Eye their kid made them that year at summer camp, they'll assume you're trying to get some work done from the road and nine times out of ten leave you alone. And on that tenth time? Take the corn muffin and tell him that God is an illusion created by man to stop the layperson from asking too many questions. Hopefully the next jackass will have orange juice.

WHAT TO FORCEFULLY ENTER IN YOUR "VERY IMPORTANT SPREADSHEET":

- As many of your friend's phone numbers as you can remember from childhood
- The lyrics to "Seasons of Love" from *Rent*
- Multiples of six
- Jean Valjean's inmate number (#24601)
- The number 69. Repeatedly.

"Misanthrope, Party of One?"—How to Eat Alone at Work

Many workers like to break up the workday with a little social interaction; the Misanthrope, however, likes to break it up with a little isolation. Working with people from nine to five is taxing enough without having to spend an entire hour in the middle of the day feigning interest in your boss's weekend antiquing plans or courtesy-laughing at whatever adorable thing the accountant's kid said last night. The average Misanthrope can only say "Oh, how lovely" twenty thousand times without cracking, and it's best not to waste these. Your lunch break is just that, Misanthrope—your lunch break. Don't feel guilty for not wanting to spend it curled up in a sleeping bag around the campfire with your coworkers, roasting marshmallows, and telling ghost stories.

Solution A: Take "French Leave"

Call it a tactical retreat. Armed with your Soup for One, hightail it out the door at 11:57. This will give you just enough lead time to slip into your hiding place without someone asking what you're doing in the stairwell/on the roof/going into the Christian Science Reading Room down the block. Your car is an excellent place to retreat to: Not only is it unequivocally "your space," but also it has lockable doors and a sound system capable of drowning out friendly little taps on the window. You can also turn it on and drive off if the tapping gets really insistent.

Solution B: Book It

An open book is the less obviously deranged equivalent of pinning a "Do Not Disturb" sign to the front of your shirt. This may open you up to a steady stream of "What are you reading?" in which case there are two sub-options: Reinforce the wall of privacy with a pair of earbuds, or tell them you're reading Ayn Rand. You may have to sacrifice one lunch hour explaining *Atlas Shrugged*, but you won't get asked again.

Solution C: Eat at Your Desk

The beauty of eating at your desk is that, for once, you actually look like a team player. You're foregoing a nice, relaxing lunchroom chat to get extra work done—you are, in fact, so busy you have to eat at your desk, tapping away between bites. If you angle your monitor away from the walkway, no one needs to know you're just playing Snood, researching the benefits of soy milk, and Wikipedia-ing "Zinc."

Wikipedia has been a boon for Misanthropes. The information may not always be completely correct, but it saves us from having to go to the library or having to ask actual people actual questions. A pound of avoidance is worth an ounce of inaccuracy.

Bullshit and Tonic: Handling Happy Hour

In China, during the Tang Dynasty, imperial servants who displeased the emperor were subjected to a particularly cruel punishment: They were forced to gather in a bar after work with their coworkers and make stiff, uninspired conversation for an hour. Afterwards, they were required to pretend they enjoyed it and to say, "We should really do this more often." Today, most workers don't have the option of begging the emperor to have mercy and cane them to death instead, but there are a few ways to ensure that your future "happy hours" are spent alone—allowing them to be legitimately happy hours.

Option AA: Putting the SOB in "Sober"

Tell them you're in recovery. If you're in a spiteful mood, (which, let's be honest, you will be) follow it with, "You knew that. Maybe you don't take my recovery seriously, but I do." If you feel ballsy enough, stand up and announce that now you have to go to a meeting, and take the afternoon off. If a coworker happens to catch you in a bar later, blame it on whomever asked you to happy hour.

Option B: Truth or Consequences

There's a Yiddish proverb: "Wine goes in; secrets come out." There's also a Misanthrope's proverb: "Three Harvey Wallbangers go in; unvarnished opinions of your coworkers come out." If no one with the authority to fire you will be at the happy hour, consider the time-honored tradition of lettin' 'er rip. Drink until you get the urge to be honest, then have one more drink to make sure your inhibitions are down for the count. Delivering slurred, bourbon-scented discourses on your coworkers' appearance, hygiene, and perceived lack of sexual prowess isn't objectively dignified, but you won't have to worry about being invited again—anywhere.

Option C: Bear Huntin'

The next time happy hour is suggested, take charge and tell them you know just the place, then lead the way across town, down a narrow alley, and behind a heavy steel door painted pink. Welcome them to Bear Down, "a nice place with a chill vibe. What? Oh, yeah, it's a gay leather and bondage bar, but it's pretty relaxed. If a guy named Austin asks if you've been bad, just tell him you're not interested. Politely." There's a substantial distance between "open-minded" and "genuinely prepared for the sight of muscular men in leather straps exploring one another," and it's safe to assume most of your coworkers will start sidling towards the door.

> "Even though a number of people have tried, no one has yet found a way to drink for a living." —Jean Kerr

I Want Custody of the Good Stapler: Divorcing a Clingy Work Spouse

What exactly is a work spouse? A work spouse is the Statler to a Misanthrope's Waldorf. The Austria to their Germany. The locked door to their drawn shades. A work spouse, in essence, is the only other person in a company of 500 employees that a Misanthrope can stand. And while it might be nice to have someone to pass "do you think my meth use is going to drive up my premium?" e-mails with during 401(k) meetings, work spouses have a tendency to get a little clingy. Suddenly the occasional snarky e-mail becomes a daily barrage of LOLcat forwards and coupons to go kayaking. A once-a-month standing lunch date turns into a daily, "Hey, when are we getting lunch?" Or worse, he wants to take the relationship outside the office with his college buddies. Just like that, your work spouse has turned into another obnoxious coworker whose e-mails you dodge like the balls he so greatly wants you to throw at his friends in a team environment after work. It's time to breakup. But don't blame yourself, Misanthrope. It's not your fault you were born this charming.

Get a New Job

Yes, it's slightly drastic, but it's effective. Usually the only thing you have in common with a work spouse is that you both hate your job, so take that away and your relationship has nothing to stand on. There are only so many times you can e-mail each other: "So, do you have a parking space at your new job?" "Yeah." "Oh, that's cool." "Yeah, it is." "Hah. Parking." "Gotta do it somewhere." "I heard that!" before whatever semblance of a friendship you had has officially fizzled out.

Set a Small (but Contained) Fire to Your Cubicle and Move to Another Floor

Proximity is another work spouse relationship killer. In the land that is Your Office, going from your desk to the kitchen is an odyssey. The floor's bathroom might as well be in Turkey for how inconveniently located it is to your cubicle. Thus, having a work spouse on another floor is like the corporate equivalent of being in a long distance relationship: You'll both try to make it work for a few weeks, but ultimately the distance is going to be too much and he'll move on to someone not separated by two long walks and an elevator ride.

Introduce a Third Party to Your Group and Odd-Man-Out Yourself

It is physically impossible for a group of friends to successfully total three people—at work or otherwise. Use this to your advantage. Or, at the very least, get yourselves into a series of kooky adventures with hilarious outcomes where everyone learns a lesson about friendship.

Famous Work Spouses in Pop Culture:

- Jim Halpert and Pam Beesly, *The Office*
- Dr. Frasier Crane and Roz Doyle, *Frasier*
- W. C. Fields and Mae West, risqué prewar movies
- Meghan Rowland and Chris Turner-Neal, *The Misanthrope's Guide to Life*
- George W. Bush and Condoleezza Rice, White House 2001–2009

The Politics of Pooping: How to Get a Little Goddamn Privacy in the Ladies' Room

Picture it: It's 11:30 on a Monday morning. You've been at work for two and a half hours and suddenly your stomach lurches, and you know that your prune Danish and IV drip of black coffee are back for a special farewell appearance. You grab your trusty Sudoku book and head to the dreaded communal bathroom, which thankfully is empty. Once in your lucky stall you settle in for a moment of much-deserved solitude and serenity. Then without warning, the bathroom door flies open and a series of impending possible nightmares flashes before your eyes — is she going to spend fifteen minutes re-doing her face? Bust out with a cheery "What's up?!" Or worst of all, sit down in the stall next to you, locking you both in a fecal Mexican Stand-Off? If chatting with your coworkers is uncomfortable, defecating in front of them is simply degrading.

The "Bronchitis Shuffle"

If time is of the essence and this is going to happen whether you like it or not, a well-placed hack or cough can mask all but the most volcanic sounds. And while a nagging cough may not be glamorous, it's better than the alternative and might even get you quarantined.

The "Royal Flush"

For the ladies' room veteran. In the bathroom, as on the dance floor, timing is everything. Just as you've reached the point of no return, flush, and let the hearty sound of an industrial water system drown all else out. True, it may waste water, but dying of thirst alone beats pooping in a crowd.

The "Promise Ring"

Like Mother always said, sometimes it's more special if you wait. As you wait, pencil skirt around your sensible work pumps, pretend like you're back in the old family station wagon with 47 miles between you and grandma's lavender-carpeted commode and count down those bottles of beer. Recite those state capitals. You can last longer than she can.

Favorite Activities for Waiting Out a Bathroom Contender:

- Memorize your pants' washing instructions (in English and Spanish)
- Organize the contents of your purse into "Made in China" and "Made in Taiwan" sides
- Create a paint-by-numbers mural on the stall door
- Toilet paper origami
- Kegels

I've Got One Hand in My Pocket and the Other One Is Busy Cleaning Some Vomit: Calling Out Sick for Nonconfrontational People

Misanthropes, by nature, are always calling out of work sick. Whether it's part of an elaborate ruse to get out of a group activity, or because solitude actually weakens the immune system, they're not afraid to dip into those two weeks of sick leave. Misanthropes are also typically a nonconfrontational people. This is problematic, as to call out of work sick, you typically have to call a superior and let them know that you won't be coming in today. Many an hour the

Misanthrope has spent rehearsing a well-written monologue about the dangers of coming into the office with strep throat, desperately trying to build the courage to hit the last number on the phone before ultimately deciding, "Fuck it—it's easier just to go in." You spend all year trying to avoid talking to your boss, Misanthrope. Now is not the time to start.

The "Just Missed You"

Everyone has a pretty good idea of when their boss typically gets into the office. The key here is to call fifteen minutes before that time and leave a voicemail explaining that whoops, you thought they'd be in by now, you must have just missed them, but you want to let them know as soon as possible that you won't be in the office today for X, Y, and Z reasons. Not only will you seem on the ball even in the face of uncertain illness, they'll feel ever-so-slightly like a failure for showing up later than you had expected. If you're feeling spicy, you can say you'll try them again later, but be prepared to think of an excuse for why you eventually didn't.

The Overachiever

Bosses across the board prefer you to call out sick rather than e-mail, but what if you're e-mailing because you're in the waiting room of the doctor's office and therefore can't call? This is a win for you on three different levels:

1. You get out of having to talk to your boss.
2. It's nine o'clock in the morning and instead of sleeping, you're already at the doctor's office trying to find a way to get better and back into work.

3. If you really were at a doctor's office, clinic, or hospital, your phone shouldn't be on at all, but there you are—breaking the rules to appease your superiors.

Warning: If you're using a home computer or laptop to send said e-mail, be sure to manually enter a "sent from a . . ." iPhone or Blackberry signature for authenticity. Don't lose it in the details; match fonts, font sizes, and colors. Odds are you're just skipping out on a company picnic anyway. You've got the time.

Phone a Friend

Con a roommate, friend, relative, or the homeless guy who lives behind your apartment complex to call your boss and pretend to be you. It's cheap, but one of your authors has done it successfully on numerous occasions and we're not saying which.

Top 10 Most Infectious Diseases:

1. Smallpox
2. Typhoid fever
3. Influenza
4. Bubonic plague
5. Cholera
6. Anthrax
7. Malaria
8. Bolivian "fuck work, there's a *Designing Women* marathon on" flu
9. Ebola
10. HIV/AIDS

Seeking Unemployment: Quitting Your Job

Deciding to quit is the easiest thing a Misanthrope will ever do, but actually quitting is much more difficult. When you decide to quit you feel free, as if the whole future were stretched out in front of you like an empty, moonlit highway. Maybe you'll finally write that novel! Learn to read Yiddish! Buy a refurbished Airstream and go West, seeing "the real America," one Indian casino at a time! You could be making handmade pottery and drinking wine in the sun like a retired lesbian dripping in turquoise jewelry, if only you didn't spend forty hours a week alphabetizing. However, the actual act of resignation is more of a challenge. Misanthropes are good at pitching go-for-broke screaming fits and great at sneaking off wordlessly in the night, but the middle ground—a calm, reasoned exchange of conflicting views—is like walking on water for us. Most Misanthropes would rather hear "There's a bomb in the house" than "I'd like to discuss this in my office," but you can sidestep this awful little "chat" with a little planning.

Get "Married"

As mentioned above, chances are good that your private life is largely a mystery to your coworkers. They don't know if you've been dating a nice Australian sheep farmer whose pasture turned out to be full of opals, encased in gold, floating in oil. (Lies are like breasts; the bigger the more impressive, and to hell with convenience.) If they ask about the ring, tell them you're having bigger diamonds put in it, "real big tacky ones." Bold men can try this approach too. It's less common, but who can say the heiress to the Pyrex fortune wasn't snared by your charms?

"And Your Little Crabs Too!"

Call a meeting. Announce that your "powers" have manifested and that you'll be leaving to pursue new opportunities terrorizing central Maryland, as Annapolis' first super villain. Change into your costume (which involves Sharpie and Wite-Out war paint and rolling up your sleeves halfway), crack the whip you've made of strung together paper clips, and scream, *"Fear the wrath of clip-chain, Old Line State!"* before dashing out the door to your Clipmobile (formerly your '98 Volkswagen Jetta).

Note that these scenarios leave an escape, so you can claim it "didn't work out" in case you need to ask for a reference later. The pasture didn't just turn up oil, but also seventeen headless corpses and you can love a killer or eat Vegemite, not both. And shit, "Did y'all know that the Naval Academy is in Annapolis? They kicked my ass in like, five minutes!"

Working Girls: How to Survive "Take Your Daughter to Work Day"

The Misanthropic woman was oddly unmoved by the Women's Lib movement. She was uninterested in suffrage, as she had no plans to wait in a line to approve of someone; abortion rights held little allure for a woman who had an elective hysterectomy at eighteen (but still uses diaphragms, just to be sure) and you can imagine her response to Free Love. You wouldn't think Mrs. Misanthrope would get tired of those long days alone with her husband at work, her solitude broken only by the purr of the Roomba and the rattle of the martini shaker, but eventually she did and went off to work with the rest of the gals. At the first office potluck, she regretted this decision deeply, but Betty Friedan smiled at her cruelly and cackled, "It's too late now, sister!" and vanished in a puff of smoke. Now not only are Misanthropic women expected to take their own little chunk out of the glass ceiling, they're expected to spend a day each year teaching the little girls in their life how to throw rocks. The next time "Take Your Daughter to Work Day" slowly dissolves into eight hours of your niece asking, "Do you always sweat that much?" here's how to transfer her to the Shut Up Division.

That's Why It's Called Work

She's just gonna find out anyway. Give her a folder, a PowerPoint file, vague instructions, and a deadline and tell her, "Just have fun with it!" Then lean forward and ominously rasp in her ear, "But if this doesn't get done by five, Mommy and Daddy might stop loving you."

Every Broken Dream Is an Opportunity

Poor Janice. So much love to give and only a Cathy mug and a bonsai to receive it. She and Tom never had children (something wrong with the pipes), and then he ran off with the consultant with the MBA and the rack to hang it on. Send your niece over and just let Jan pretend for a while. She's got some Life Savers in her purse.

The Wicked Stepmother

"Now remember, princesses take all of their NyQuil!"

> ### INAPPROPRIATE "TAKE YOUR DAUGHTER TO WORK DAY" STAND-INS:
>
> Your father's much younger mistress, Craigslist escort, a schoolyard bully, a mason jar full of lice, a female impersonator (working on his "Shirley Temple"), enough candy for all but one of the children

Damn, Everybody Knows My Name: The Danger of Being a "Regular"

When the majority of your workday is spent fantasizing about dental school and toeing the line between "lazy blinking" and full-blown REM sleep, getting out of the office can mean the difference between a clean record and explaining "aggravated assault with stapler and piss-poor attitude." Whether it's the fresh air or the comfort of being surrounded by others who are miserable at their jobs, nothing rejuvenates like taking a trip to the deli downstairs to grab a quick nosh. It's the intermission in the god awful high school production of *Annie Get Your Gun* that is Your Work Day. Having your familiar deli, though, comes with a price: The staff starts to think of you as one of their "regulars" and suddenly you're the guest star in *Sandwich Follies '11*. You may not want to participate in this daily song and dance, but there's no such thing as a free lunch. Here are some of their classic numbers.

The Playfully Difficult

Deli Guy with dreams of vaudeville stardom: Heyyyyyyy! Look who it is, huh?

Misanthrope: Good afternoon.

Deli Guy: What can I get ya, sweetheart?

Misanthrope: Can I have a B.L.T., please?

Deli Guy: Oooof, wish I could, honey, but we're all out of bread today.

Misanthrope: This is a bakery. You have 80 pounds of bread directly behind you.

Deli Guy: What, that bread? *Pauly!* When did this bread get here?! You're making me look like a putz in front of Julia Roberts! Hey, I'm just funnin' ya, kid. One club sandwich coming up.

Misanthrope: Oh, I said B.L.T., actually.

Deli Guy: You heard her, Pauly, one *turkey reuben!*

Misanthrope: Look, I'd love to stand here and do Lucy at the Sandwich Shop with you all day, but I've got a meeting in five minutes; can I just get my B.L.T., Ethel?

Deli Guy: Oooh, ouch! Kitty's got claws! Alright, alright, that'll be $14,000—special heartbreaker tax, today only!

The Spanish Inquisition

You know when you get home after a long, hard day at work and your significant other asks you how your day was, and you feel like you might snap into two distinct, but equally annoyed pieces because everyday is the same and the same is horrible, so why in God's name do they insist on asking over and over and over again? Well it's just as annoying when you do it, Sandwich Guy, and you're not even going to go down on me later when we're both too tired to have sex but know something's gotta give.

The Sorority Sister

"Yes, I'd like the sandwich again, no I don't want to 'switch things up,' and although I only took Spanish for two weeks during sixth grade, I'm fairly certain *punta gorda* doesn't mean 'coming right up, ma'am.'"

Better idea: Get Chinese every day. They only care if you want it for here or to go, and MSG makes your hair shiny.

Chapter 4

A ROSE ON THE PILLOW, A CIGARETTE BURN ON THE SHEETS

{ Sex, Love, and the Misanthrope }

There's something intrinsically undignified about love, and sex is downright embarrassing. At the stroke of midnight, every Cinderella turns into a bag of fluids and feelings, and all the glass slippers in the world won't shut her up. Nevertheless, every now and then Cupid shoots wide and hits a Misanthrope. It's not pretty, but occasional intercourse is a better way to release tension than making little cities out of Silly Putty and smashing them flat with your fist.

Button Will Pop Up If Seal Is Tampered With: Losing Your Virginity

Most Misanthropes are fairly skilled lovers. Unafraid to take what we want and unlikely to derail a partner's orgasm with a whispered "I want to be one with you," Misanthropes shine in the seedier sexual situations, leaving behind a trail of barroom anecdotes beginning, "Oh, man, this one time at the oil change place . . ." These short-term victories aside, however, some Misanthropes have a hard time quelling the gag reflex long enough to perform what is laughably called "the act of love." The erotic prerequisite of feigned interest in a potential bedmate's "career" at Burger King is a stronger inhibitor than a phalanx of teaching nuns, and some of us just can't get past it. If you're having trouble sealing the deal, here are a few potential solutions.

The Sure Thing

Find a mid-sized town and go to the Applebee's on Friday evening, when the bar will be near capacity with divorcees on the rebound and guys with pinky rings. Find a good prospect, sit down, and tell him the truth over a few Death by Chocolate Fudge-a-Tinis. It may be awkward at first, but the same "me first" mindset that made Neil Armstrong elbow Buzz Aldrin and jump down ahead of him, combined with the barfly's relief at a no-crabs guarantee, will all but ensure success.

Hail Mary Pass

Consider taking the veil and joining a religious community. You've come this far, and many orders guarantee a vow of silence and your own cell. Make sure you join a monastery with a history of seclusion, though; you don't want to find out you've signed up for an order that sends out missionaries or, worse, teachers.

Hustle 'n Go

It's not the most dignified approach, but you can always hire a professional. Consider this: Whores hear it all. Even ignoring the very real dangers sex workers face, they get asked to do or say any number of batshit crazy things. Imagine the relief they'll feel on seeing the car window roll down and hearing, "I want you to have intercourse with me in a prompt, businesslike manner. Please don't make any small talk, or any talk not immediately germane to the matter at hand." You'll be their best fare of the night.

EUPHEMISMS FOR LOSING YOUR VIRGINITY:

Popping your cherry, reducing the resale value, accepting applications, the grand opening, pawning the promise ring, solving the puzzle, divide and conquer

---

Thanks for the Sex, Now Get Your Sweaty Leg Off Me: How to Avoid the Post-Coital Cuddle

Loath as we are to admit it, and as much as our actions may suggest otherwise, Misanthropes are people too. As such, we have the normal range of human needs: food, shelter, an occasional "just because" pedicure, and yes, despite its cooperative nature, even sex. After the twitching subsides and the final grunts die down, you're left with a serious problem—several dozen pounds of sweating, farting, breathing, yammering, emotional person in your bed, marking your sheets with its scent. And worse, it wants to cuddle.

Aggressive ("Advance!")

As a guest in your house, your partner is allowed freedom of movement only within certain clearly defined areas. If a limb flops over the mid-bed Maginot Line, flop it back. If they roll toward you, roll them back, all the way onto the floor if you have to. If your "activity partner" is larger than you, you may have to brace your back against the wall and push with your legs, but a strained muscle is a small price to pay for the defense of one's personal space.

Passive-Aggressive ("The Bachman-Turner Overdrive Defense")

Invest in a small battery-operated stereo, and swing by a church bazaar to pick up a selection of Amy Grant cassettes. When you find yourself ensnared by your partner's sweaty tentacles, quietly slip out, go to the closet, pop in the "Baby Baby" single and put it on as loud as you can stand. When The Bed Monster inevitably wakes, smile apologetically and explain, "Oh, that's just my neighbor, Vlad. He's having a *hard time*. It's . . . it's best not to disturb him when he's like this," and hope your erstwhile bedmate leaves before you have to turn the cassette over.

Actual Violence ("The Nuclear Option!")

She doesn't know you don't have night terrors. Especially if this is her first time sleeping over. So wait until your partner drifts off to sleep, then go to your Dark Place and channel a weeping four-year-old boy in urine-soaked X-men pajamas. Think about the failure of your fourth grade flute recital and slug your unwanted bedmate in the beak while screaming, *"El avestruz! El avestruz del diablo!"* Smooth over the inevitable, "What the hell??" with, "Sorry, night terrors! Have 'em all the time!" and drift off with the reassurance that next time she'll be sure to keep her distance.

> ### OTHER BANDS VLAD IS REALLY INTO RIGHT NOW:
> Pat Benatar, Rush, Papa Roach, Everything But the Girl, The Mighty Mighty Bosstones, Harvey & the Wallbangers, Wilson Phillips, New Kids on the Block, and Jefferson Starship

Three's Company: The Misanthrope and Group Sex

On the other side of the coin, there are times when you're left with too much of a good thing. A few too many Chardonnays, the phrase "I'll try anything once," and a worryingly long cab ride, and suddenly there you are—there they are—and it dawns on you, with ever-mounting horror, that you've agreed to join a group. It's your week of ill-advised improv classes all over again. It all seemed so harmless at the bar, but now the two of them (oh, God, let there be only two) are there, naked. Beckoning. Ready. Misanthropes can handle unorthodox sexual behavior, but a threesome is too much like a team sport. Get out of the tangled mess by putting yourself on the bench.

Do a Phenomenal Job

Reach for the stars. Call on every *Cosmopolitan* cover you ever glanced at, every bathroom wall you ever read, and turn in the performance of your life. Remember that enthusiasm can often cover for weak technique, and that all those stories about "hours of passion" aren't representative—most people simply want to have an orgasm with minimal fuss, then catch a *Mad About You* rerun before dozing off. If you do well enough, you can get everyone done in twenty minutes, and be in a cab home in under half an hour.

The Amy Winehouse Defense

Al Gore can say whatever he wants about carbon emissions; the truly inconvenient truth is that vomit is the universal reset button. Generalized "feeling bad" didn't get you out of going to school, nor did impassioned shouts of "*I hate the other children! Homeschool me!*" No, to stay home from school, you had to throw up. Bosses expect you to shoulder on with a cold, coaches want you to "push through" the pain of an injury, but if you puke it's agreed that the party's over, the day is done, and it's time to say goodnight. You've already drunk too much. Merely make one too-rapid movement, and you'll be able to play the human body's most decisive trump card.

Paper Covers Rock

Tell them to go ahead, and you'll play the winner. Slip out while they try to decide what constitutes "victory."

**DISTINCTIVE MASKS TO WEAR TO
A HIGH-CLASS ORGY:**

Gerald Ford, luchadora, high school mascot head (go Cats!), detoxifying seaweed, Groucho Marx glasses and nose, Dora the Explorer, cut from the back of a cereal box

---

"That Seems . . . Excessive": What to Do If You're Not Into That

There's a lot out there for a Misanthrope to not be into so this is going to come up. Cases in point:

- Sex swings require the athleticism and flexibility of a Chinese gymnast with a gold medal.
- Bondage induces claustrophobia.
- Role-play belongs in the social worker's office and not in the bedroom.
- Feet are what God gave us to remind us we're disgusting.

- Handcuffs make it impossible to run away without taking the entire bed frame with you.
- Sadism is a coping mechanism (not a fetish).
- The packaging for those edible panties says they're made in a facility that also processes peanuts, and you're not taking the chance.
- A lady's ass is for marriage, sir.

Before he gives you a lot of "free to be you and me" horseshit about trying new experiences and being "open," strap one of these on and go to town.

Tell Him That That's How Your Parents Died When You Were in the Sixth Grade

While the odds are pretty high that it won't make entirely too much sense or be factual in the very least, nothing trumps in an argument faster than being an orphan and he'll never be able to enjoy the act again without thinking, "Wait, how did this kill two people?" Forensic puzzles during sex are like a torpedo aimed directly at the *U.S.S. Sustained Erection*.

Tell Him You Can't Because You're a Vegan

Bonus: then he might break up with you!

Do It, but Sigh Heavily and Tap Your Foot Impatiently the Entire Time

Remember how your mom acted at the New Kids on the Block concert? Well, you didn't ask her to take you to the Tiffany concert next year, did you? You may have to ask Dr. Ansory to squeeze you in next week, but he won't ask you to do it again. Not with that attitude.

So, You Think You Might Be Gay

The hints are beginning to pile up. You prefer soccer to football, which you try to blame on a genetic throwback to a European grandmother, but which really might have to do with the fact that the football uniforms don't ride up over the players' meaty thighs. The effeminate cashier at the deli always coyly mentions "extra meat" when you come in, and hands you your change in a certain lingering way. You've begun to really "feel" disco, all the women at work have been telling you their problems, and, arguably most convincing of all, you've amassed an enormous collection of homosexual pornography. Even that guy who sleeps over all the time is starting to get suspicious. If you think you might be gay, here's what you should do.

Step 1: Experiment

What else is your first semester at NYU for?

Step 2: Experiment Some More

Maybe mom's right; maybe you are just doing this to hurt her.

Step 3: Enjoy It While It Lasts

Slather on the body glitter, join a gym with one treadmill and ten empty rooms, and order the boys another round—you've got about five years until last call. You're getting more rights whether you like it or not, and soon not even homosexuality will save you from stumbling blindly into the matrimonial bear trap and ending up a trophy on parenthood's wall. Circuit parties are almost impossible to enjoy when you know you have to be home by 8:30 to read *Goodnight Moon* to Mai Ling, so wear out those hot pants now before they cause a stir at the PTA.

Step 4: Don't Turn Into One of Those Feelings Queens

No one likes a forty-five-year-old Nellie crying into his Shirley Temple at the bar because the director's commentary for *Philadelphia* hit too close to home. It makes us all look bad.

Step 5: Retire and Open a Bed and Breakfast in Vermont with Your Golden Retrievers (Partner Optional)

What else are your twilight years for if not sun-drenched walks down country lanes, tax-deductible antiquing, counseling newlyweds on patience, fires on cold nights, apple cider pressed that morning, sending anecdotes to the *Reader's Digest* humor column, curling up under grandma's afghan, tai chi on misty mornings, enjoying a glass of wine on the deck as you reflect on a life well lived and take in a glorious sunset, fussing endlessly over the house, and twinks—lots, and lots of twinks.

So It's Come to This: Creating The Misanthrope's Online Dating Profile

If you haven't had sex since Deee-Lite was climbing the charts, the HOV lane shaved a good 20 minutes off your commute, and your grandma offered to pay—you're officially ready to enter the world of online dating. But don't worry Misanthrope, if by the grace of God something actually works out, you can always just tell people you met on Craigslist.

Handle

"ItsWaterW8"

Picture

Although it's tempting, don't use that post-mono super-thin pic that's been welcoming people to your Facebook profile since 2006; there's a difference between "flattering" and "deceptive." Also avoid using the "wacky picture" of you with a bong on a polar bear skin rug—you're trying to get a date, not a callback for a regional production of *A Funny Thing Happened on the Way to the Forum*. No props, no sidekicks, no stage makeup; just look at the goddamn camera.

About Me

If you're tempted to write "Just ask ;)" you might as well have your mom write it. At least she thinks you're handsome.

Interests

Do not be that guy who alphabetizes a list of his 200 favorite bands (Peaches, Pitchshifter, Pixies, Presidents of the United States of America . . .) or thinks anyone cares that he's concentrating on his delts this month. Also come to terms with the fact that we, as a people and a nation, enjoy cooking, travel, and spending time with friends. Move on and think outside the box. Which would catch your eye more: "long walks and Pilates" or "reorganizing my Netflix queue and going to the gym drunk?"

Favorite Book/TV Show/Movie

You catch more flies with honey than vinegar and you can catch more fly honeys (we're so sorry . . .) with Nicholas Sparks/*Family Guy*/*Hot Tub Time Machine* than Bret Easton Ellis/*Twin Peaks*/*Drop Dead Fred*.

Perfect Date

For every old sock, there's an old shoe—there has to be someone out there who wants to give you a blow job while you play video games and watch NASCAR.

Looking For

If you want a thick girl who'll do it on a hardwood floor, then just come right out and say you're looking for a thick girl who'll do it on a hardwood floor. Euphemisms just waste time (besides, we all know "a girl who doesn't take herself too seriously" is code for someone who doesn't expect expensive dates).

What You Learned from Your Past Relationships

"It turns out RussianBrides.com doesn't offer financing options and my Yahoo chatroom girlfriend was a robot."

IN CASE ITSWATERW8 IS TAKEN:

2sexy4LSU, SassyAnglBB_1973, ThatsWutSheSaid69, CreedFan267, UtahDentist, R8dNC-17, ScienceDude3.1459, Looking4Beard

---

Skip to the Dirty Parts: Getting Laid Without the Small Talk

In the animal kingdom, mating is approached with a business-like detachment achieved only through eons of Darwinian pressure. Birds perform mating displays, not "Do you want to get coffee sometime and talk?" displays. If a boy bear approaches a girl bear in the forest, it's not because he thought she must be deep if she was reading Camus while swatting salmon out of the stream; it's because he can tell by the scent of her urine that she is in estrus and it is go time. Fish needn't even touch! They just spray their business over the streambed, have a cigarette, and get back to their mahjong. But of course humans, inventors of the traffic circle and post office, don't follow this common sense approach. We've foregone the straightforward ritual of smelling each other for the much more unpleasant ritual of hours, if not days, if not weeks of small talk. If the adorable, evolutionary cul-de-sac that is a Boston terrier can close the deal in under an hour, shouldn't you be able to?

Tell Her You're Shipping Out Tomorrow

Hell, it worked for our grandparents.

Pretend You're on a Scavenger Hunt

Walk up to her with a long list in your hand and explain that you're doing a scavenger hunt and all that's standing between you and a $25 gift certificate to iTunes is a quick grind in the John. Sure that list is actually just an old receipt from Jiffy Lube with "Bieber Fever" written on it over and over again, but she won't notice. It's amazing the things people are willing to go along with if it helps the team—just look at suicide bombers and defensive linemen. If she wavers, offer to use part of your gift card to buy her Sufjan Steven's new album, *Missouri Loves Company*.

Pretend You're Tom Wopat

If there's anything women love more than Sandra Bullock movies and a two-for-one deal at Macy's, it's banging their way down the Hollywood Walk of Fame. Lucky for you, it's dark and Tom Wopat ain't been in much recently. Blue up your eyes with contacts and adopt a hearty swagger. Walk over with the confidence only a Hazzard boy could pull off and say, "Hey baby. I'm Tom Wopat. You may remember me from TV's *The Dukes of Hazzard* and the hit sitcom *Cybill*? Christine Baranski? A doll to work with. Anyway, how about you, me, [grab your junk] and Boss Hogg here step out to the General Lee and get into a whole mess of trouble?" If she turns you down, you can always just get ripped with Cooter.

OTHER CLASSIC TV STARS YOU COULD PASS FOR IN THE DARK:

Burt Reynolds, Paul Michael Glaser, Erik Estrada, Russell Johnson, Patrick Duffy, Ted Danson, Don Johnson, Meshach Taylor

---

R U REDY 2 CUM?: The Misanthrope's Guide to Sexting

Sexting is the preferred substitute for bumpin' uglies for two distinct groups of people—fifteen-year-olds and Misanthropes. Teens like it because they can do it at the dinner table and youth group lock-ins, whereas Misanthropes appreciate any form of intimacy that can be done alone, in silence, and with an unobstructed view of Anthony Bourdain's masterful, dominant profile on the flickering screen. What Yahweh did for Judaism and Tyler Durden did for fight club, we've done for sexting: Lay down the ground rules.

Rule #1: Never Send Naked Pictures of Yourself

Receiving is fine, but sending? Absolutely not. It's hard to feel superior to that bitch at Panera when you have eight blurry crotch-shots of yourself on your T-Mobile prepaid phone.

Rule #2: Keep It Light

When two people start swapping text messages about how desperately they wish the other were here right now, they're standing on a slippery slope leading directly to a pit of meaningful emotions. Declarations of love or any serious relationship-defining talk should *never* happen via text message. Not because with those matters face-to-face communication is important, mind you, but just because it's uncomfortable and downright embarrassing and then there's a record. You know, in case things get all "courtroom."

Rule #3: Don't Say You're Into Something When You're Not

Because a few months down the line when you're both actually in Tampa at the same time and he rented a saddle and bought a bag of carrots, man is your face going to be red.

Rule #4: "Come" Is Spelled With an O, Not a U

You're not twelve and this isn't an AOL chatroom.

Rule #5: Double-Check Who the Message Is Going to EVERY Time

Because "Dad" is close to "Dan" and Sunday dinner is going to be real awkward if he knows his little girl is wetter than a tile saw.

Rule #6: No, You Don't Want to Call and Listen to Each Other Come

If you're going to listen to his grunting climax, you should just move into a doublewide and celebrate your common law marriage.

FIELD NOTES:

Him: where U at

Misanthrope: I am at my home, sir.

Him: wanna fuk

Misanthrope: Alas, I cannot. I'm going on a day cruise down the Rappahannock tomorrow and need my rest.

Him: send pic of ur tits

Misanthrope: Negatory.

Him: boobies 4 cock

Misanthrope: This isn't a swap meet.

Him: my dick is so fing hard

Misanthrope: And my legs need to be shaved; we all got problems.

Him: r u touching urself

Misanthrope: Sure.

Him: oh fck im gonna cum

Misanthrope: Well, thanks for playing.

The Parent Trap: How to Avoid Meeting Her Parents

"Hi, I'm Chad and I'm going to be taking care of you today during your awkward, introductory brunch with your future in-laws! Would you like me to tell you about our prix-fixe brunch? For starters we have hollow cantaloupe that's been filled with a medley of strawberries, honeydew, and stilted conversation. That's going to be followed by crepes made with your choice of fruit, Nutella, or a searching, unblinking stare. Next up we have a selection of some lovely scones, crumpets, and passive-aggressive comments that don't help anyone. Our main course this morning is eggs Benedict served on a bed of mutual disdain and seasonal greens. To drink we have your choice of teas, including Earl Grey, English breakfast, and 'so you fucked my daughter?' And of course if you want something harder, we offer bloody marys, mimosas, or your choice of benzodiazepines. I'm just going to give you a few minutes to think that over, and I'll come back when you look like you're ready to admit defeat and go back on JDate." Never again.

Only Date Orphans

This was considerably easier in Industrial Revolution era London when soot and tuberculosis kept the life expectancy under the voting age, fingerless gloves were all the rage, and a gallon of homemade gin only cost a shilling. (Man, those were the days . . .)

Only Date Immigrants

This solves the parent problem and the chitchat problem in one fell swoop. If it turns out your girlfriend has been saving her tips from her job at Lao-Town's second-biggest piano bar and wants to fly you back to Luang Prabing to meet the whole dang gang, officially change your name to "Mohammed Al Islam" and let the No-Fly List take care of it for you. Thanks, Uncle Sam!

Only Date Spoiled White Chicks with Daddy Issues

Whether she's a drugged-out trustafarian or a hardcore gender warrior, everything she does is motivated by her need to piss daddy off (it's nice to piss mom off too, but it's the patriarchy that really gets her pronouns in a twist) and bringing home a Misanthrope will only score her two "no daughter of mine!"s and one "I shouldn't have sent you to Sarah Lawrence!" She'll figure if it barely gets her compared to her sister (the one dating a Swanson, of the Hungry-Man Swanson's), it's not worth the train fare to New Haven.

PET NAMES FOR DADDY:

Phallocentric Fascist, oppressive wife-owner, authoritarian bureaucrat, antiwoman dollar-monger, bourgeois Reaganite, gas-guzzling peniscrat

No Thanks, I Already Ate: What to Do If You're Proposed to in Public

There are some events in your life that while important, shouldn't necessarily be done in a public forum. For example, yearly pelvic exams are important for women's health, but they should be done in the doctor's office with the door closed, not at Yankee Stadium on free pretzel day. Masturbation happens alone on your couch watching *Silk Stalkings*, not at the airport. If you can grasp this concept, why can't your would-be fiancé? Proposing to a Misanthrope in public is as rude as giving a vampire a guest pass to Palm Beach Tanning. As if the public emotions weren't bad enough (and they're pretty fuckin' bad), you're surrounded by dozens of people, all fixing you with a moist expectant gaze. An older woman clutches her husband's arm and mouths, "Say yes!" across the way, as everyone holds their breath and waits for a fairytale to begin. Unless you're marrying a die-hard *Rocky Horror* enthusiast, a marriage proposal should not involve audience participation. When your heart says no but the peer pressure says yes, here's your battle plan.

Ring in the Champagne Glass at a Restaurant

Bottoms up! That should buy you a few days of "processing time."

At a Family Function

Redirect: "*Mom drinks!!!!*"

In Nature

Promise God you'll go work with the poor in Calcutta if, just this once, he sends *bees*.

New Year's Eve

"Ooo, this is awkward . . . my resolution was to bag a doctor."

On a Beautiful Bridge in Venice, Where Lovers Have Met and Cemented Their Love for Millennia

Jump.

On the Jumbotron at Halftime, Packers Lead Bears by Six

Slug the guy to your right and scream, "*Who dat!*" (That makes people riot, right?)

If you really love your Misanthrope and want to spend the rest of your life with her (when she can stand it), it's important to propose in the calmest, subtlest way possible. Compose a "no pressure!" telegram and send it to her P.O. box. She'll get back to you—eventually.

"Buy her a shot; she's getting married!!!": The Misanthrope's Bachelor/ette Party

Bachelor and bachelorette parties are easy to get out of when they're for your friends (you're allergic to glitter, you're having elective surgery, your dog won't let you—the possibilities are literally endless), but it's not so easy when it's your own. As the guest of honor, you need to show your face and no matter how many acupuncture appointments you make, they just keep rescheduling so it's "convenient" for you. Meet them halfway: Go ahead and let them throw you a party, but insist on some veto power.

Avoid:

- Strippers: You might as well save yourself the money and crowd surf in a petri dish
- Strip clubs: Nothing says "celebration!" like four-dollar steaks and the heady aroma of hepatitis and Windex
- Porn: Has your future brother-in-law ever seen you try to conceal your erection with a two-month-old copy of *Good Housekeeping*? Well, now he has. Welcome to the family.
- Stripperobics: Nothing's more boring than an ex-whore trying to go respectable
- Crying: Here's a Kleenex and some poppers; try to pull yourself together, girlie
- Novelty veils, sashes, or crowns: It's a bachelorette party, not the "We're All Winners!" runners-up brunch at the Miss South Carolina pageant
- Phallus-shaped anything: Get it? It's a penis straw!
- Destination bachelor/ette parties: I can be as embarrassed here as I can be in Key West, but at least here the cab ride will be cheaper

- Party busses: The vehicular embodiment of a barbed wire tattoo
- Mardis Gras beads: Unless your friends really want to hear your FEMA rant again

Agree to:
- Lots of alcohol, and a call girl with a kind face fresh off a Z-Pak
- Two words: *Risk Party*!
- *Night Court* marathon and a big ol' spliff

> ### REASONS TO REFUSE A LAP DANCE WITHOUT SEEMING GAY:
>
> - I just got my suit pressed
> - My leprosy's acting up
> - Not big on asses, thanks
> - I'm just not that into you
> - I have a daughter about your age
> - I just requested "Wind Beneath my Wings" on the jukebox and don't want to miss it

To Love, Honor, and Evade: How to Avoid a Big Wedding

You got out of your bat mitzvah by accepting Christ, only to reject Him again just in time to dodge confirmation; you got out of your deb ball by playing "Anything But" with your escort in the parking lot instead; you got out of your high school graduation ceremony by failing Spanish and stealing a projector; you got out of your twenty-first birthday party by admitting you have an alcohol problem; and you ditched your college commencement by going to "find yourself" in Sweden instead. You've been the James Bond of opting out, dodging every bullet that comes your way. But uh-oh, here comes Grace Jones with a tire iron—you're getting married. That means an endless round of meetings, events, swatches, meetings, events, swatches, all culminating in a public declaration of emotions while wearing a too-tight ball gown in the most universally unflattering color, in front of God and everybody. Your antisocial curmudgeonry has been disappointing your mother for your entire life; she really should have seen this coming.

Elope to Vegas

Drive through wedding chapels, no blood tests, and four miles of all-you-can-eat buffets—the better question is, why *wouldn't* you get married in Vegas? Sometimes a Joan Rivers impersonator licensed by the state and $10-worth of chips says "I love you" more than self-written vows read from tear-stained notebook paper ever could. Plus, Britney Spears, Kim Kardashian, and your white trash stepsister did it, and look how well it worked out for them!

Plan a Destination Wedding

Book a week at Sandals Algiers, include an embossed list of recommended vaccinations with the save the date, and tell your friends not to change their money just yet—the dinar has been doing some wacky shit lately. Everyone loves a wedding, even the rebel forces.

Get Married at an Anime Convention

Because your friends like you, but not nearly enough to dress up like a school girl/cat hybrid with a "power gauntlet" and throw Pocky when the minister announces you man and wife-chan.

Don't Get Married

Don't compromise a solid FICA score just because he thinks you're "The One." He cooks a mean pot roast, but can you really love a man who defaulted on his custom Kawasaki?

POPULAR MISANTHROPE ANIME SERIES TITLES:

Super Happy Funball Alone Hour!, Greg + Vampire!, Isorate!, Kiss Kiss Cave Time!, Mermaid Privacy Rodeo!, Divorce Primetime Shuffle 3½!, Pan-Pacific Suicide Jamboree!

It's Not Me, It's You: The Misanthrope Ends a Relationship

If a Misanthrope can barely work up the nerve to check her voicemail after skipping a dental appointment, is it any surprise that she'll do anything to avoid the emotional Waterloo of breaking up with someone, including staying married for 60 years to a man who genuinely believes that Kurt Cobain was murdered? The conspiracy theories were cute at first, but when he thinks he can prove it, it's time to make a creative exit before you spend the rest of your life listening to Hole's *Celebrity Skin* album backwards for hidden clues.

Drop Off the Face of the Planet

When Amelia Earhart woke up one morning and realized she loved George Putnam but wasn't in love with him, she didn't just change her e-mail, return his favorite Wilco T-shirt, and ask for her keys back. She covered her tracks so well, no one in America knew her new phone number or if she'd moved on yet. When Jimmy Hoffa looked back on forty-three years of marriage and saw only nagging and dry casseroles, did he tell the Teamsters to take five while he and Josephine went to couples therapy and learned to use "I statements"? No, he turned himself into a fucking *building*. It's not for the faint of heart, but it works. Only avoidance that extreme can completely protect you against late night "I'm thinking about us" text messages and unstable "I was just in the neighborhood" workplace visits.

Death by a Thousand Snips

"Sorry I was late, I was busy cheating on you. Don't worry though, we mostly used a condom." "Oh shit, are these instant mashed potatoes again? Gross, I'm going to have dinner at Rhonda's; she's a better cook than you anyway. Leave the door unlocked because I'll probably be pretty wasted by the time I get back. Don't worry, I'll wake you up if I want a quick BJ." "PS: I noticed you've been gaining a little weight lately, so I threw out your antidepressants. You're welcome." They'll either breakup with you or they'll let you get away with anything, and either way . . .

Floor It and See How Long It Takes Him to Bail

On your one-month anniversary, casually say, "No pressure, but it's almost harvest time and dad needs to know if he should slaughter the hogs or save them for my dowry. They're a little rangy, but sturdy in the hoof."

THE REST OF YOUR DOWRY:

The deep freezer that works but makes that weird sound, a gently used air hockey table, a 1995 Mazda Protégé with Nova Scotia tags, a wide array of decorative gourds, a Garfield beach towel, 5,000 Confederate dollars

Chapter 5

I GAVE YOU LIFE AND I CAN TAKE IT BACK AGAIN, WITH INTEREST

{ The Misanthrope as Parent }

Try these on for size: womb, birth canal, fetus, amniotic, placenta, dilation, cervix, umbilicus, birth coach, lactation, mastitis, forceps, episiotomy, "It's crowning!" Doesn't that just make you feel . . . sticky? It's funny how a friendly game of "Just the Tip" can turn into twenty-six hours of backbreaking pain, a taint ripped asunder, and decades of fiscal and emotional responsibility. If you don't want to pull a "Prom" and leave it on the steps of the local fire station, here's how to handle the tangible aftermath of one glorious night in the back of a Camaro.

He's Not the Only One You'll Feel Kicking: When Strangers Touch Your Pregnant Belly

Pregnancy is terrible. Weight gain, bizarre cravings, and hormone-driven mood swings kept the cartoon character "Cathy" afloat (unfortunately) for decades, but they're even less funny in real life. The pregnant Misanthrope has another concern: For nine months, it is technically impossible to be alone. Discounting the baby—it may wriggle and press on various organs, but it can't speak yet—pregnancy nevertheless invites a lot of company. The checker at the store wants to know how far along you are. The bus driver wonders if you're hoping for a boy or a girl, and the teller at the bank postpones putting your transaction through to tell you about how terrible it was when she gave birth—it was in backwards, you know, and they had to use forceps, which for her explains both the child's eventual transvestitism and her own incontinence. Worse, your body goes from defended to indispensible in the twinkling of an eye, as passersby stop to feel your taut belly and meditate on the majesty that is reproduction. Not only is this achingly, maddeningly rude, you have to pee, again, and you have to detach these womb-crazed navel-gazers *fast*.

Turnabout Is Fair Play

They're treating you like a brood mare; treat them like a pure-bred greyhound on an auction block. Check their fingernails, pull up their lip to get a look at the teeth, and if you feel like driving the point home, give their breasts and/or genitals a heft in the palm of your hand. Give your pronouncement: "Not much for breeding, I'm afraid. Paltry udders and an overall bloodless look. Decidedly inferior stock, but may be serviceable as a house pet or a filler animal in a manger scene. I hope you didn't pay much."

"Let Go of Her, You Bitch!"

Sometimes, it's worth the trouble to do an extra-good job. Though most people use this argument to encourage their cleaning ladies to really *get at* the oven, it applies equally well to misanthropy. Make the investment, and have a special effects artist rig you a portable, lightweight version of the parasitic larva from *Alien*, complete with blood squib and wriggling action. Insist that it be activated by a pocket-sized remote, weaken the seams in the front of your maternity blouses, and never leave the house unarmed again.

> You can only do this once, but it's a doozy: Have your water break all over them. Zinger!

My Body, My Self: How to Give Birth in Relative Privacy

In most cultures, in most contexts, a woman who bares her genitals while screaming obscenities is considered either a witch or a sought-after entertainer. In either case, this is not misanthropic behavior, since cooch-to-the-wind hollering is sure to draw a crowd. Whether the onlookers have stones or dollar bills is beside the point: they're still there. Somehow, though, birth has come to be considered a group activity, and if she's not careful the whelping Misanthrope may find herself surrounded by the father, the midwife, the doula, the doctor, several supportive relatives, some passersby who heard the noise and stopped by to see if a party was going on, some guy with a camera phone who "seems harmless," and the lady with the alligator purse. This is a lot for even the most open-minded Misanthrope, but even under duress you can bring the numbers down.

Golden Opportunity

How often have you wanted to throw something directly at someone's head? How often have you had the excuse, "I'm expelling a person from my body in fulfillment of an ancient Biblical curse?" It's not rocket science. Most of us have to keep our misanthropy in check almost all the time; if you're in a situation where you can get away with kneecapping someone with an IV stand, you should do it.

"Sorry about the Upholstery"

Wait as long as you can, then take a cab to a hospital across town. If you time it well, you can birth in transit—just you, your baby, and a recent immigrant from an even more recent country. This approach can also lighten the burden of choosing a baby name, since you can name the child after the road or bridge you were on and the cabbie. Verrazano Mehmet will grow up with a great story, and you won't have to explain to your pothead sister why her suggestion of "Doobs O'Nugget" is a terrible name.

The Hippie Hippie Shake

Judo experts are able to use an opponent's motion to flip or throw them; apply this approach to the "togetherness" logic behind having a crowd at birth. Tell everyone that what you really want is for the birth to be a personal bonding experience between you and the baby. It's the first time you're really meeting, see, and you'd hate to invite a lot of people the baby doesn't really know, because that's rude. Ideally, you can stretch this out for days or weeks—it takes a long time to really cement that bond.

MEHMET THE BIRTHING COACH:

"Do you need me to pull or tug anything? I think there might be some aspirin in the glove compartment; that might help? Don't worry, my mother had me at a bus shelter and I turned out just fine!"

I'll Give You Five Dollars to Pretend to Believe in the Stork: Having "The Talk"

"Daddy, where do babies come from?" Like "Do you love me?" and "Did you use my toothbrush?" there's no good answer to this question. There's the truth, which involves frank discussion of the various movements of fluids and, arguably more alarming, love. Then there are lies, which are generally unconvincing, and if creative enough may technically constitute abuse. The time-honored solution is to punt to the other parent, but if this meets, "She told me to come ask you, and to tell you that if she had to do it, you could at least explain it," you can try any of the following tricks.

Ayn Rand's Fairy Tales

It's never too early to reinforce the capitalist ideal. "Babies are available at most department stores. As with hair dryers, you get what you pay for; unlike with cars, it's usually more convenient to buy American. Now go read your children's illustrated edition of *The Fountainhead*."

Georgia O'Keeffe, Medical Illustrator

Tell the truth, but do so with as much use of metaphor, allegory, and floral imagery as possible. God willing, your child will be in no hurry to act on "the urges of the pineapple." You'll also be spared the discomfort of looking directly into your child's eager, trusting face and saying, "At this point, under normal circumstances and provided that reproduction is the ultimate goal, the gentleman will insert his erect penis into the lady's expectant vagina."

The Decline and Fall of Western Civilization, Silver Lining Department

Let your child use the Internet unsupervised for two hours. He may come away with unrealistic expectations, but he'll damn sure have figured out the nuts and bolts of "insert tab A into slot B." If your child is studious, you may have to block Wikipedia for this to work, or you may be faced with "Daddy, did you know that giant ground sloths once roamed South America? Oh, and don't forget you were going to tell me about how to make babies."

WORST EUPHEMISMS FOR GENITALS:

Down there, Whoopsie-doodles, Sand pocket, Rascal Flatts, Party Platter, *The Secret World of Alex Mack*, the Oot

---

Spiked Punch and a *Reader's Digest* Condensed Book: Passing Time at Children's Birthday Parties

At a certain point in your early thirties your friends start pumping out kids with Mormon-like zeal and regularity. Suddenly every weekend you find yourself sitting around a sheet cake with a bunch of parents, nodding mechanically at another discussion about nanny cams and autism. You'd love to stand up and walk away, but the last time you strayed from the other adults, parents started looking at you like you were a trench coat and a doll collection away from Megan's Law registration. You're tempted to stop coming to these altogether, but free cake is free cake and it's your only chance to indulge your secret passion for musical chairs and goodie bags. But look on the bright side: At least none of those pancake-batter-covered nightmares belong to you and you don't have to spend the entire party screaming, *"Taylor—that's too high!"* and wondering if you remembered to bring the EpiPen. Now is the time to enjoy your freedom and make your own fun.

Chat Up the Guy in the SpongeBob Costume

Because he's even more uncomfortable than you are and God only knows what's under that giant, plush head.

Beat the Shit Out of the Piñata and Revel in Your Hulk-Like Strength

You're finally the strongest person in the room and this isn't going to happen again until your early decision application to a retirement home, so act now. Fling the tots aside (they weren't doing much damage with their little chicken arms anyway) and come down on that candy-filled cardboard ballerina harder than the Julliard audition committee. (Ballerinas have no business being full of candy, anyway.)

Call Your Gynecologist and Discuss Birth-Control Options

Do it now while it's on your mind.

If You Can't Beat 'Em, Join 'Em

You washed that cake down with Pepsi and now you're all hopped up on sugar—better burn it off now before you have a temper tantrum in the parking lot and get sent to the time out chair. Swan dive into the ball pit and backstroke your way through the lost socks and startled children. Better a raging case of pink eye than hearing anymore about Kayleigh's new gluten-free diet.

> **THINGS WE FOUND IN THE BALL PIT:**
>
> A drawing of Harry Potter rescuing Timmy from gym and taking him back to Hogwarts (where he belongs), a clarinet, asbestos, a lot of half-sucked Jolly Ranchers, $5.71 in change, a Trapper Keeper, a D-spelling test with "ketchup" spelled with a backwards R, Hailey's meds, a pair of light-up sneakers, too many retainers

"Ms. Diane Put Her Cigarette Out in the Goldfish Bowl!": How to Get Fired from Being Homeroom Mom

An education degree does not prepare most people for the reality of classroom teaching. Sure they can say "self-esteem" in 80 languages and write a dissertation on the limits of good touching, but crowd control isn't a core course in the education program at SUNY-Albany. They cover this deficit by recruiting a core of unpaid, Pinot Grigio powered riot police, alternatively dubbed Homeroom Mothers. If you get drafted for this duty, here are some easy ways to get out of it without shooting yourself in the foot.

"Why Do You Ask, Two Bears Screwing?"

Racism: It got you excused from jury duty faster than you can say, "Africa's that way, Kizzy," so put on your sheet and try again. On Native American History Day, stroll up to one of the children's work groups, straddle one of their tiny chairs and say, "*How*, children. I'm Henry's mom, Ms. Diane, and I'm going to save us all a lot of time and trouble and teach you the plight of the noble Red Man in seven quick steps." Then, as you belt out your best war whoop, pantomime an arrow shot, throw your hands up in surrender, tip back a bottle of "fire water," shoot craps, count your imaginary money, and end it all by slitting your wrists. As they escort you out of the building, protest, "No, it's okay! I'm a 1/16 Blackfoot!"

WIC Approved

When it's your turn to bring in the class snack, peel open a packet of bologna and walk down the aisles slapping a slice down on each desk muttering that you hope no one's on a low-sodium diet. Do this every time until it's just too sad.

Smoke Unfiltered Chesterfields

"I *think* I have enough for the whole class . . ."

Knots Landing Elementary

If two kids get in a fight on your recess watch, stand back and watch with mild interest as you light up another Chesterfield. When a responsible adult breaks up the fight and confronts you about your laissez-faire attitude towards school bullying, reply evenly, "It's really Kelly's fault, she's been leading them both on."

History 101 with Ms. Diane:

- "Ulysses S. Grant. Nice boy. *Always* drunk."
- "Oh no honey, we didn't land on the moon; that was an outtake from *The Outer Limits*."
- "Let's skip the Boston Tea Party because that was boring. Now the Stonewall Riots—best Goddamn sweet sixteen a girl ever had!"
- "So then Randy Quaid flies his little ship into the big ship and blows it up, all the aliens die, Will Smith ends up with Vivica A.

Fox, and Bill Pullman's approval ratings have never been higher. And that's why we celebrate Independence Day."

Four-Foot-Three and Pregnant with a Heart Condition: How to Get out of Going to the Amusement Park

The fifteenth-century Flemish painter Hieronymus Bosch depicted hell in his most widely known triptych, *The Garden of Earthly Delights*, as a dark underworld dripping in vulgar and surreal imagery like disembodied appendages, demons, bloody corpses, heretic pigs, and disturbing animal hybrids, as an ominous warning of what will happen if you give in to the Devil and his temptations. Almost 600 years later, American blogger Meghan Rowland depicted hell in her most widely ignored Microsoft Paint creation, *The Fairgrounds of Dehydrated Heatstroke*. In it, you'll find an amusement park on a Saturday afternoon in August, packed with long lines, fried foods, rotund eight-year-old boys wearing their T-shirts around their necks instead of where they belong—on and covering their ample breasts, whiplash inducing rides, and everywhere flip-flops. She painted this masterpiece to warn Misanthropes of the horrors of agreeing to chaperone the fifth-grade class trip. Art historians still argue about which depiction is more terrifying, but one thing is for sure—you'd rather be eaten alive by a giant bird hybrid than go back to Six Flags.

Trick Someone Else to Take Them

Are you sure you can't sign your own children up for the Big Brothers Big Sisters program? I mean does it really matter if your terrible addiction is to *True Blood* and not heroin?

Take Them to the Houston Public Library and Tell Them It's an Amusement Park

"Oh children, there are wonderful rides! With books you can battle monsters on Mars! Sail with bloodthirsty pirates on the high seas! Rescue princesses from fearsome dragons! And it's air-conditioned and won't cost me a thing! Because it's in your imagination! And if you get tired of reading, you can ride the escalators up and down for four hours! Now Daddy will be in periodicals catching up on *National Review*; don't make eye contact with the homeless people."

Hard Truths

Drive them to an empty parking lot across town, tell them it got torn down, and go home. Since they're already having a bad day, maybe you should go ahead and tell them the truth about Santa, the Easter Bunny, and the extreme unlikelihood of Gerbil Heaven.

OTHER AMUSEMENT PARK STAND-INS:

Mormon temples, the county courthouse, a nearby community college, LAX Airport, Chinatown, Barnes & Noble, the pediatrician's office, Lane Bryant

Your Kid Is Being Bullied and You Have to End a Motherfucker: Misanthrope as Mama Grizzly

Misanthropes are painfully easy targets for schoolyard bullies. There's nothing particularly likeable or cool about being the kid who insists on wearing ski gloves while holding hands with his bathroom buddy, brings "existentialism" every week to show and tell, and automatically responds to "Tag! You're it!" with "Touch me again and I will scream." But at least you took your ostracism like a man—by escaping in *X-Files* fan fiction and developing an impressive tolerance to paint thinner fumes from hiding so often in the art room. If only you had passed that kind of bravery onto your kid instead of a predisposition to diabetes. Little Johnny is getting picked on in school and now he wants to stay home with you everyday. You were willing to cut him some slack in the beginning and allow him a few "mental health days," but now he's starting to seriously get in the way of your yoga exercises and affair with the mailman. As if that wasn't bad enough, today you found a home-schooling brochure in his backpack. It's time to get protective.

Fuck the Bully's Mom

Literally. Have sexual intercourse with his mother.

Gender Warrior

Sneak into the bully's house and pull a pharmaceutical *Freaky Friday*. Switch Junior's Ritalin with mommy's hormone replacement pills, and send him barreling through puberty in the wrong lane. As his breasts swell and his moods swing, he won't feel like hot shit for much longer—not with a nickname like Tearful Tommy Tits-a-Lot. But his mom will drop weight like a bulimic with a tapeworm and zip through the crossword!

Beat the Living Shit Out of Him

It's fast, it's effective, and it's only your second strike.

Just Get Your Kid to Stop Dotting His I's with Little Saturns Already

"Your mother and I love you, but he has a point."

WHAT TEARFUL TOMMY TITS-A-LOT TOOK AWAY FROM A CLOSE READING OF *ARE YOU THERE GOD? IT'S ME, MARGARET*:

Puberty can be a scary time, but it's natural and it's nothing to worry about. Everyone gets her period at a different time, and there's nothing to be ashamed of, one way or the other.

Compensating for Rickets and a Lisp: What to Do If Your Kid Is Lame

If you had an obvious taste for privacy but no obvious physical or mental defects, chances are you're still remembered fondly, if inaccurately, by people you went to high school with: "Yeah, Chris Turner-Neal. He did his own thing. Slept with the principal's wife instead of going to prom." I actually went to prom with the girl who chain-smoked in the parking lot, but they remember me as having done something cooler. To our eternal dismay, Misanthropes are only human, so this skewed adulation often goes to our heads and we start believing we're cool. All is roses until you have a child who gets kicked out of his Dungeons and Dragons group for "lowering the tone," and who brought an orchid to show and tell. Sir, Madam, your child is lame.

Send It Away for Repairs

Anyone who tells you that boarding schools exist to give a good education is as big a liar as someone who tells you boarding schools exist for the social prestige. Wealth can buy many luxuries, one of which is the ability to send your child to have its acne and feelings years in another state. After several years away, your child will have either grown out of the awkward stage or become a dedicated Misanthrope—finally giving you something to talk to each other about.

Lie Your Ass Off

Through whatever means you can think of, spread a rumor about your child that will make them cool in the eyes of their peers, like it or not. If you have a daughter, the quickest way to the other girl's hearts is through a tiara, so make up a lost kingdom and plop her down as its princess. With a son, anything will impress the other boys if it's disgusting enough. An honored classic is to claim that he was originally a twin, but absorbed his sibling in the womb, and at any point he might find his brother's tooth growing out his armpit . . .

Plan 420

Let him smoke pot. It's not a great card to play, but three of a kind beats a pair, and "stoner" beats "lame."

Did You Hear?! Menudo Played Her Quinceañera!

What to Do If Your Kid Loves a Shitty Teeny-bopper Band

Once upon a time you were the aloof but sexy Tower Records clerk in the leather miniskirts and Doc Martins who knew about every cool band three weeks before everyone else. You never had to show your ID to get into shows, and you were once at the center of a rumor involving a public indecency arrest, an empty bottle of Boone's Farm, and Perry Como. Fifteen years and an asleep-at-the-switch IUD later, you've just paid $185 to watch five prepubescent boys from Pensacola gyrate their hairless bodies for a crowd of 40,000 screaming tweens and gay men while you hope you'll be able to get up in time for work tomorrow morning. Why, oh why, couldn't she have been born deaf?

Pretend to Like Them Yourself

To a tween, nothing is less cool than your mom—all she thinks, all she touches, all she is. If mom were an outfit, she'd be a sleeveless burgundy mock turtleneck paired with high-waisted, pleat-front, elastic-backed jeans with tapered legs, Keds, and clip-on earrings. If you casually pick up the CD case and comment, "Oh, these boys! Your mom likes to jam out to them in the car on the way to jazzercise!" Suddenly they'll seem as cool as an animal print dickey. If enough moms do this, the band might even breakup.

Take One for the Team

Remember that time you landed on the front of the *Richmond Gazette* when a photographer snapped an unfortunate picture of you at the Tears for Fears concert shouting *"Play 'Head over Heels'!"* and the editor thought it complemented the headline "BRITISH NEW WAVE BAND 'RULES THE WORLD'!" perfectly?

Find it. Bring it to your daughter. Point to it. Point to her. Point to it again. Look her in the eyes and matter-of-factly say, "You look like an asshole and everybody in your generation has camera phones." If she mentions them again, start ominously humming "Mad World."

Psychological Warfare

Invest in a pair of soundproof headphones, lock her in her room, and blast the band's number one hit on a loop for six days straight. It's drier than water boarding and less tiring than beating her with a rubber hose.

> **Tracks from P-Town Princes' new album, *2 Hot 2 Panhandle*:**

- "Gurl"
- "O Gurl Y"
- "Save Me a Seat in Civics"
- "U + It = DAMN!"
- "Did You Really Join Model UN?"
- "If I Could Take SAT Prep for My Heart (You Would be My Tutor)"

No One's Good Enough for My Little Girl, But Especially Not You: When You Hate Your Child's Significant Other

Almost as appalling as your child's progress through puberty is its eventual results. Clad in pheromones and newly-minted pubic hair, she'll start trying to pair off with other teenagers, hoping to find out what second base is and to get there, in either order. It's safe to assume you won't like whomever your child dates, since teens are almost as obnoxious as people. Many cautious parents will try to outlast their child's infatuation, relying on the notoriously short adolescent attention span. However, if your little one's sweetheart is just too revolting to be borne, you can speed the process.

Good Old Bribery

One of them will dump the other for a price you can afford. You may have to haggle, you may have to try each one in turn, but one of them will crack for a few dollars. There may be a teenager somewhere who loves a high school sweetheart more than a case of Keystone Light and some new electronics, but there aren't two. If possible, get bids from both and go with the cheaper one—you're a Misanthrope, not a fool.

"Your Mother and I Love You, No Matter What"

The tragic state of America's public schools ensures that your child has a grasp on science that is shaky, at best. Call your son into the kitchen, sit him down, and have a serious talk: "We had you tested at birth, and I'm afraid the results were very clear. You're gay. I know this must come as a surprise, but your mother and I love you very much. You may want to tell that girl who's always here—she deserves to know." It may confuse him for a while, but by the time he does a little disappointing experimenting and comes back with more questions, the awful girlfriend will be long gone.

The Devil and the Deep Blue Sea

This one is messy, but foolproof. Invite the unwanted beloved over for a good old-fashioned summer barbecue. Dress in black robes, top the ensemble off with a horned headdress, and tie a goat to a short stake in the back yard. When Junior's plus-one arrives, hand her a dagger, and tell her that as the guest, she gets to "go first." In the unlikely event that she actually takes knife in hand and moves toward the goat, all you need say is "You get to carve the watermelon, not Captain Goatsworth! What kind of freak are you?"

Your response when your son comes back six months later, furious, shouting that not only did he find out there's no such thing as a blood test for homosexuality, but he just fingered a girl on his friend Jesse's couch and it was "rad": "Jesus Christ, it was just a joke."

They Use the Same Physics in Norway, Dammit: Helping Your Child Choose a College Far from Home

Eighteen years is a long time. If you're a Misanthrope, it may be the longest relationship you've had with someone other than your probation officer. As much as you presumably love your child, she's still there. You offered to sign the emancipation papers every birthday since she was twelve, but she always giggled and said, "Oh, Daddy, you're silly." You've been very patient, but now it's time the apple fell far from the tree.

Finally, I Can Really Perfect My Greenlandic

Encourage every strange intellectual whim your child has, keeping in mind that certain interests can only be pursued in situ. Archaeologists spend months on digs, and anthropologists can spend years among isolated tribes. The jackpot field is international relations: Your child will be so busy getting both sides of the story in India and Pakistan, Israel and Iran, and a baker's dozen of feuding African states, he'll barely even have time to ask for money.

Spread Your Wings, Little Bird

Have a nice "fatherly chat" with your daughter. Weave a yarn about how she's leaving the nest and must soar . . . soar *all* the way across state lines, and how proud you are to have raised someone who's so unafraid to move all the way across the Mississippi to follow her dreams. If you have the pipes, don't be afraid to round this off with a heartfelt rendition of "Climb Every Mountain." She'll leave inspired, confident, and itching to get away from a father who punctuates arguments with show tunes.

12,000 Sitcoms Can't Be Wrong

Reverse psychology is a revered plot point in television for a reason: It occasionally works. "College-bound young lady" is a dressed-up way of saying "teenage girl," and teenage girls love to spite their parents. Three or four mentions about how you'll be so lonely if she goes farther away than Down-the-Road State should do it.

A U-haul and a Dream

Misanthropes often have excellent credit, since bill collectors love to talk. You're not likely to be terribly attached to wherever you live, so if your child doggedly refuses to move past the feasible-to-come-home-and-do-laundry line, pick up stakes and move yourself to one of those faraway-sounding frontier towns like Coeur d'Alene or The Dalles. Get a post office box once you get there — you want to stay in touch, but don't want the kid just popping by like the Avon lady.

OTHER SHOW TUNES IN DAD'S REPERTOIRE:

"Cell Block Tango" (with character voices), *Chicago*, "Ease on Down the Road," *The Wiz*, "Bosom Buddies," *Mame* (with a Bea Arthur sock puppet)

Honey, Don't Put That Rhinestone in Your Mouth, You Don't Know *Where* It's Been: If Your Child Is in a Beauty Pageant

Who knew that your little Ashley would avoid inheriting both your deviated septum and your husband's port wine stain (the one shaped like Alfred Hitchcock's profile) and turn out to be a cute kid? Unfortunately, when her day care held a cautionary screening of "Toddlers and Tiaras," she completely missed the irony. Before you could say "unrealistic standard of beauty," her *father* had already taken Ashley to the mall and signed her up for the local children's beauty pageant. Here's how to make sure she doesn't shame you by winning "Miss Congeniality."

Embrace It

"Pageant mother" is English for "bitch," and that's a role you're used to filling. Change Ashley's name to "Ash-Leigh" and paint the town Ramsey. Buy a few sets of matching mother-daughter hair extensions, Clorox her pearlies, and add an edging of sequins and rickrack to everything she owns. At the pageant, cheat like a drunk evangelist. Pull a Tonya Harding and kneecap a promising rival contestant with her own fire baton. Win over the male judges (in the unlikely event you get a "straight vibe" from any of them) by flashing them ("One breast now, the other after you give her a perfect score"). You can't lose: Either you embarrass Ash-Leigh so badly she refuses to participate, or your hard work pays off and she brings home a tiara and a $45 gift card to Red Lobster.

Treason: It's for Her Own Good.

Coat the bottom of her tap shoes with a thin layer of baby oil — she won't so much "Shuffle Off to Buffalo" as fall on her ass in Carson City.

Temporary Disfigurement

The object is to affect her appearance enough that she won't do the pageant, but not so badly you could charge neighborhood kids a quarter to look at her. Adjust all the seams on the left sides of her garments so that she's constantly pulled into a gentle but noticeable lean, and point out that princesses never tilt. If you're afraid this will lead to a visit from the Scoliosis Fairy, simply slip into her room at night and apply an enormous, politically charged henna tattoo to your daughter's sleeping form. No matter how on-beat her tap routine is, all the judges will see is "U.S. OUT OF KOREA!" across her forehead.

TOP PHRASES HEARD SHOUTED BACKSTAGE AT THE LI'L MISS CARSON CITY GALLERIA PAGEANT:

- "Don't suck the Vaseline off your teeth, it might stunt your growth!"
- "Sequins cuts are part of being a woman. Be strong."
- "Don't touch anything! Your spray tan isn't dry yet!"
- "You may *not* begin puberty before the end of the pageant season, Missy."
- "MADYSEN! BE NICE!"
- "Cinderella didn't practice *her* shuffle ball chains either, and that's why she was poor."
- "Feminism is for ugly girls. Now go steam your crinolines."

Chapter 6

OH, GO, ALL YE FAITHFUL

{ Holidays with a Misanthrope }

If God walked among us, do you think he'd celebrate his son's birthday by giving a box set of the TV show *Perfect Strangers* and a $10 Bath & Body Works gift card to a distant relative whose name he pulled out of a "Gone Fishin'" hat? No. Because: 1) omnipotent and 2) it's stupid. He'd rather be watching a twenty-four-hour *Matlock* marathon and eating a whole Russell Stover sampler box by himself, but if a Misanthrope does the same thing, he gets called "Scrooge" and told to "get in the spirit of the season." With corporations cranking out new holidays as fast as their greeting card poets can write, the Misanthrope has to be armed against festivity the whole year 'round.

We're Here, We're Queer, and We Have Something We Need to Talk to You About: National Coming Out Day

"I Have Something to Tell You." This *never* prefaces good news. No one has ever said, "I have something to tell you. Here's $7,000," or "I have something to tell you. You smell like flowers." National Coming Out Day, a twenty-four-hour period of "I have something to tell you" alternating with "I feel so free" and "I'm not ashamed anymore!" is the Misanthrope's Appomattox. Loners who can face war, famine, pestilence, and death with equanimity and grace fall like wheat before a scythe when their coworkers and neighbors come up to them and say, "I have something to tell you. I haven't been honest with you, or with myself . . ."

One-Upmanship

I'll see your gay and raise you treason. Nothing takes the wind out of someone's sails like a good solid one-up, so after your mailman comes out as a homosexual, you come out as a Red agent. "I know just how you feel! My real name is Sergei Alexandrovich Kharovsky. I've been living here incognito for twenty years, working to undermine the United States and her interests abroad. It feels so good to finally be honest. Would you like a vodka?" (Remember to pronounce it *wodka*.) If you'd rather be dead than Red, consider telling him you're transsexual, dying, or a vampire — or, if necessary, all three.

Awkward Is as Awkward Does

Feign complete ignorance. "What exactly is 'gay?' I hear about it so often on the TV, but no one ever explains." Once they tell you, ask a series of increasingly graphic questions about "How that actually *works*." They said they wanted you to know . . .

Politely Refuse

"I'm sorry, I don't mean to be rude, but I just don't have time. I know you people are looking to shore up your numbers and that you have heavy recruitment quotas, but work has been very hectic lately and I barely even have time to hand-pick all the bugs off my heirloom tomato plants. You know how it is."

Make an Offensive Joke

Immediately pull the fire alarm. When questioned about it later, say, "I'm sorry, I saw something *flaming*." What the hell, life is short, and you may not get many chances.

WHEN THE MISANTHROPE COMES OUT:

Just don't, and go on about your life as usual. If your same-sex exploits come up in conversation and someone says, "Oh, I didn't know you were gay," fix them with a steely gaze and answer, "Yes, you did. I sent out a memo two years ago. Don't you ever check your spam folder?"

Cupid Flew Into the Bug Zapper: The Misanthrope on Valentine's Day

Misanthropes raised as Christians always have mixed feelings about Noah's Ark. The planet-clearing flood is the star of the show, of course, and often inspires hours of creative play in which the young Misanthrope builds an elaborate civilization in the sandbox, then goes for the hose. It's the pairing off that's so hard to get behind. The Misanthrope's hatred of groups often includes a revulsion against simple pairings, which explains why Misanthropes who've been married for decades will still introduce their spouses with, "This is my, uh, friend Valerie." Valentine's Day doesn't so much frighten Misanthropes as disorient them: Talking to a Misanthrope about how badly you want to "find someone" or how happy you are to have "found someone" is like describing color to a blind man. The Misanthrope may not be asked on a sunset hot-air balloon ride, but that doesn't mean he'll be bored.

Like Bird Watching, but Crueler

Go to the supermarket, pick a spot near the frozen foods, and hunker down. Sooner rather than later, you'll begin seeing the night's victims straggle by, mascara and dignity in ruins, eager to fill the void with sweet, comforting ice cream. Make sure you listen to the mutterings as they pass: "*Ice cream* doesn't think we're in two different places right now. *Ice cream* doesn't think I'm pretentious. *Ice cream* doesn't only date girls who do anal." If you wait long enough, you may even see a tall, expensively dressed man in his middle years open the freezer door, place his head among the cartons, and begin to weep.

Fish in a Barrel

It's easier to get laid on Valentine's Day than at a Roman orgy. 2-for-1 drink specials and the woman's boundless ability to be disappointed by men ensure that by 10 P.M., the streets will be filled with furious ladies wobbling on their stilettos and looking for a hate-fuck. Hide your sharp objects, spray on some Old Spice, and go take your pick.

Schmalentine's Day

Gather all your single friends together for a "FEH, who needs 'em?" movies, mojitos, and "Mystery Date" night. Once they arrive, announce that you can't stay because you have a date, but they're welcome to whatever's in the fridge.

IF YOU HAVE A VALENTINE:

If you have a valentine this year, don't suggest that you each go have your own Valentine's Day and report back, and whoever had a better time gets to choose the scenario for the next role-play Tuesday. It sounds like a good idea, but it's not.

Kisses Flavored with the Rich, Hearty Aroma of an Eggnog Belch: What to Do if You're Caught Under the Mistletoe

Misanthropes love to stand in doorways. If you need to escape an impromptu sing-along, you're already halfway gone, no one can come chat with you without blocking the entire walkway, and there's the added bonus of safety in the event of an earthquake. Eleven months out of the year, this works just fine, but come December a doorway is the worst place a Misanthrope can be, because it's mistletoe season. Kissing under the mistletoe may be the most objectively absurd Yuletide tradition. God sent His son to earth so that mankind's sins can be forgiven, so let's celebrate by hanging a sprig of greenery from the transom and letting a distant relative who insists that "it's not incest if it's between *third* cousins," use it as an excuse to walk in a few singles? Ingrid means well, and she's probably legally correct that nothing in Arizona law stands between the two of you, but that doesn't mean you have to stand there and take it like a public drinking fountain.

Wham, Bam, No Ma'am

The instant she touches you, let out a power yell and sucker punch her in the gut as hard as you can. Apologize, explaining that your reflexes have gotten extra sharp since you've been taking Krav Maga. She's lucky, in a way: Had she been three inches taller, the blow might have killed her.

Spice It Up

Train yourself to have an inhuman tolerance to spicy foods; then always have a jalapeno in your mouth. When Ingrid locks on, push it forward into her mouth with your tongue. In the few seconds before the heat registers, she'll hopefully think you're playfully sharing a Werther's Original and greedily suck the pepper in.

Like an Eighth-Grade Dance

Be a terrible kisser. Stick your tongue in her mouth and leave it there like a forgotten umbrella; lick the side of her face with a loud slurp; clamp down on her upper lip so hard you draw blood. Once bitten, twice shy.

Just Don't Play

Take the mistletoe down the minute you come in the door. You're a fully-grown adult Misanthrope, and you don't have to play "Seven Minutes in Heaven" just because it's Christmas.

Other Stuff to Carry in Your Mouth, Just in Case:

- A mousetrap
- Live bees
- A big ol' wad of chaw
- About a tablespoon of kerosene
- A handful of potpourri
- Iron filings
- A raw oyster

Eating the Miniature Krackles Yourself: How to Dissuade Trick-or-Treaters

A pack of trick-or-treaters is not ultimately much different from a Viking raiding party, what with screaming bands of marauders swooping down out of the night demanding tribute. While medieval peasants in undefended coastal villages may have had little choice but to take one for England, you, the modern American Misanthrope, can fight back. You may annoy a few parents, but if they weren't willing to buy their children candy themselves, they should have known to expect some bitterness with the sweet.

Rain Dance

The resourceful Dutch have traditionally repelled invaders by opening the dikes that protect their low-lying territory and letting the North Sea do their dirty work for them. You may not have the might of the oceans at your disposal, but you can have a powerful sprinklers system installed and linked to a convenient indoor switch. Wait until the little tots are most of the way up your sidewalks, then turn on the waterworks and watch them scatter.

Instead of Candy, Distribute Informative Pamphlets

Instead of the fleeting, fattening pleasure the children would get from candy (a moment on the lips, a lifetime on the hips), wouldn't it be much sweeter for the kiddies to be warned against little-known health risks and enjoy a longer, more productive life? When they ring your doorbell, hold out their pillowcases and plastic pumpkins, and cry "Trick or Treat!" Give them each a copy of *Radon Abatement Strategies for the Concerned Homeowner: A Free Publication of the Cuyahoga County Department of Health and Human Services.* It comes with a coupon for a free one-hour Geiger counter rental!

The Old Radley House

It's easy to forget what morbid, perverse little creatures children are. Every neighborhood with a few children has a designated "scary" house, whose inhabitant is reputed to be a witch, cannibal, or white slave trader. Take on this role with an occasional well-planned act for the benefit of the children. Leave a bloody rag sticking out of the side of your garbage can, and let the shrubs in front of your house die. Every once in a while, go into your back yard and sob, "Oh, *God,* what have I become? *Why can't I stop?*" If you do this too often the neighborhood's adults will start to get suspicious and you might have to have another awkward tea with Officer Dan, but if they're spaced just right you'll be given the supreme accolade, "Scary Old Mr. Turner-Neal." You can put it on your mailbox.

Radon is an odorless, colorless noble gas with atomic number 86 and is produced by radium decay. It is highly radioactive, and in some cases homes built on radium-rich soil can fill with high concentrations of radon, increasing the inhabitants' risk for certain cancers. For more information, visit *www.epa.gov/radon.*

The Bunny Hop: Cheerful Neighbors Have Hidden Easter Eggs in Your Yard Again

Your neighbors just don't understand. You called the police on their block party, screamed unimaginable blasphemies when they came to the door caroling, and only do yard work in the wee hours to avoid their robotic bleats of "Howdy, neighbor!" and yet still they come, with the implacability of a panzer unit, trying to get you to participate. They seem to think that if they can just try hard enough, sweetly enough, *long* enough, they can crack open your shell and scrape aside the meat to find a beautiful, friendly pearl. Maybe if you were to look out your window and see the neighborhood children laughing and frolicking as they scampered across your lawn hunting Easter eggs, your icy heart would melt and you would come to know the joys of community.

No dice.

"Oh, Gross, This Horse Is Full of Greeks!"

If the eggs are the hollow plastic kind that are meant to be opened and filled with candy and treats, you can have a lot of fun turning each one into a little springtime Trojan horse. Between when the parents hide them and the children are turned loose to hunt, gather them and take them inside. Replace the candy with odd or disturbing things—you can try to get creative, but really nothing will work as well as a good old-fashioned assortment of garden pests: out go the jellybeans, in goes a centipede; so long, chocolate footballs, pleased to meet you, miller moth; down with marshmallow eggs, up with pill bugs. The little girls will squeal, the little boys will be delighted, and the parents will learn to use the vacant lot next year, poison ivy or no.

Finders Keepers

Spear the eggs like so many Styrofoam cups on the median, dropping those you find into a sack at your belt. Take them back inside and eat them while taking a long, relaxing bath, ignoring the pounding on the door and the muffled shouts of "You're ruining it for everyone!"

The Guy at the Pet Store Is Getting Suspicious

You know what eats eggs, moves faster than a child, and will startle the hell out of someone not expecting to see it? Ten iguanas. The minute you see those chubby little legs churning towards your property line, open the cage and shout, "Scuttle, my pretties!" Twenty years later, you can expect thank-you notes from area psychologists who have grown rich reassuring these children, now grown, that swarms of lizards are a rarity in the developed world.

The Iguanas' Names:

- Roscoe
- Miss Boom-Boom
- Hortensia
- General Murgatroyd
- The Gipper
- Cleopatra
- The Great Green Hope
- Blitzen
- Miami Todd
- Shop-Vac

Why Is This Night More Tedious Than All Other Nights?: It's Your Turn to Host the Seder

Being "chosen" is seldom a good thing. Diners *choose* a lobster from the tank to steam and devour. Psychiatric patients *choose* a parent to blame for their borderline personality disorder. Great Britain *chose* to make India a colony. The Jews have gradually learned what Misanthropes have always known instinctively: To be singled out is to be in danger. Shortly after God *chose* the Hebrews, the Egyptians *chose* to enslave them, having *chosen* to be remembered for enormous pyramids they didn't *choose* to build themselves. God then *chose* to liberate His people and lead them to a land He had *chosen*, which was a convenient forty-year desert trek away. Four thousand years later, your family has unaccountably *chosen* you to host the annual commemoration of these events, but you can certainly *choose* to make sure it never happens again.

Show and Tell

Increasingly, museums are incorporating interactive exhibits that allow their patrons to feel more connected to the history. Your family has probably never actually seen a wrath-of-God plague in action—shouldn't they, so they can *really get into* their heritage? Fiery hail and dying livestock may be a little labor-intensive, but you can go to the pet store and fill up on frogs and crickets (an acceptable stand-in for locusts), and darkness is only a trip to the breaker panel away. Turn this plague sampler loose, and your relatives will be edging toward the door long before you ask, "Now, which of you was born first? I forget . . ."

Be "That Guy"

Every teenager has a year during their "earnest" phase when they try to ruin Thanksgiving by constantly reminding everyone how badly it ultimately went for the Indians, and then screaming *"Native Americans!"* at anyone who says "Indians." This Passover, take Pharaoh's side. "He had to get the pyramids built somehow! And what would you do if your contractors just decided to go to Israel before your tomb was finished because there were 'too many locusts' and 'God told them?' You'd go after them, dammit."

A Shande far de Goyim

When your family arrives, be stretched out on the couch with an ice pack and a glass of Alka-Seltzer, nursing a brutal hangover. "Listen. About the Seder, I may have gotten into the Manischewitz a little early this year and sort of . . . not done anything. I'll order us some meat lover's pizzas and put on a 'Best of Don Rickles' DVD. It's the best I can do, unless you want to go wrap my Egyptian neighbor's house."

Other Jewish Holidays About Narrowly Averting Extermination:

- Purim
- Hanukkah
- Tisha b'Av
- Yom ha-Shoah
- Yom ha-Zikaron

Malls are for Elderly Power-Walkers and the Teenagers Who Work at the Orange Julius: Holiday Shopping Tips for the Misanthrope

Misanthropes have accepted that they must buy holiday gifts. We've come to regard this as an annual, unavoidable excise of money and patience, sort of an "Income Tax II: The Reckoning." The shopping is the brutal part. Since most Americans have never directly experienced famine, catastrophe, or the privations of war, we have to manufacture nightmarish, traumatic events to serve as bonding experiences. This is how Black Friday came to be. Ordinary, relatively sane housewives who think the annual Running of the Bulls in Pamplona is dangerous, reckless, and cruel to the bulls, will stampede to strip malls the day after Thanksgiving, flattening any who dare come between them and the all-important, life-giving *Sales*! Black Friday shoppers will do things for a discounted salad spinner that they wouldn't do to save their own mothers from the firing squad, solely for the joy of sitting around at Starbucks later and talking about how terrible the whole experience was, how long they waited in line, and how they'll never do it again. This is the Misanthrope's idea of hell. As much as he enjoys seeing humanity at its worst, no earthly force could compel a Misanthrope to join these lunatics. Online shopping is the obvious solution, but if you're still boycotting Overstock.com for their come-in-your-face *O Is for Orgasm. Get It?* ad campaign, here are some backup plans.

What's So Touching Is That You Made It Yourself!

Learn a craft and make everyone gifts by hand. Your new hobby can be one that produces fairly conventional gifts, like homemade jam, but need not be: Taxidermy is easy to learn, and the look on your mother's face when she unwraps her raccoon will become a treasured holiday memory for everyone.

You All Needed One

Buy everyone the same item. Go to your local bulk retailer and ask to look at things that are sold by the pallet, and load 'er on up. You're done in one stop, no one can claim they don't have an iron and need to borrow yours, and no one can make a stink about how their gift didn't cost as much as someone else's.

Do Your Shopping at the ATM

No one's gonna say no to $20. And if they do, keep it.

Shit You Can Crochet:

- Oven mitts
- Body stockings
- An enormous afghan depicting Washington crossing the Delaware
- A prom dress
- Wildly impractical Maxi Pads
- Slipcovers for every single object in the house
- A surprisingly cozy shroud
- A *hideous* bikini
- Skorts

Dropping the Ball as the Ball Drops: New Year's Eve

Not every Misanthrope hates every holiday. Repeal Day, the December 5th celebration of the day Prohibition ended, is always a winner, as are those nonholiday days off like Memorial Day, Columbus Day, and Labor Day that don't come with obvious party themes. Unfortunately, these few easy-to-manage red-letter days don't come close to making up for the darkest day on the Misanthrope's calendar: New Year's Eve. The next time your sociable friends beg you to come to their countdown soiree, show them this explanation of why you'll be at home, reading comic books with a flashlight under the covers, and ripping through an Entenmann's sampler.

All This "Fresh Start" Nonsense

The idea of New Year's Eve being "a chance to start over" doesn't impress a man who went to four colleges in four years, transferring every summer because the RAs at the last place were too chummy. Misanthropes quit jobs, move, and change banks at the drop of a hat and get several dozen "fresh starts" a year. *It's what we do.* The only thing special about "starting fresh" on New Year's Eve is that everyone else is doing it too. You wouldn't care if someone became a pescetarian in April or got a new haircut in October; why should you have to hear about how they're making their own bread just because it's December 31st?

Pucker Up

More than any other holiday, New Year's Eve demands physical contact. You can get by with a handshake on Yom Kippur and a fist bump on Cinco de Mayo, but New Year's Eve centers around finding someone clean-looking by eleven, talking to them about Modest Mouse for an hour, and then letting them suck on your tongue as the temporal odometer rolls over "to start the new year off right." Stay home and give your dog a peck on the snout instead; his breath won't be much worse, and he doesn't own an "I Only Date Liberals" T-shirt.

Everybody Asks You Your Plans

And they won't take "mind your own Goddamn business" for an answer. You can spend Juneteenth alone and stay in on Diwali and no one bats an eye, but admit that you don't have plans for New Year's and suddenly everyone feels sorry for you and invites you over, which just compounds the problem.

A MISANTHROPE'S RESOLUTIONS:

To find the person who first said, "Live fast, die young, and leave a beautiful fucking corpse," and slap him silly. Keep up with yoga.

Let Freedom Ring: Independence Day

It's not American independence that bothers you—it's the way the whole process is commemorated that you find overwhelming. There's a lot of outdoors, a lot of group picnics, and a lot of gap-toothed children busily eating hot dogs and smearing ketchup and mustard across their faces like war paint. Come evening, as the mosquitos roll forth en masse to feast on logy revelers, the high school choir will sing a few patriotic songs as the onlookers gently sway, like reeds stirred by the gentle winds of liberty. The whole she-bang is ultimately topped off by a fireworks display, which combines the jarring sound of repeated explosions with the bovine "oooh . . . ahhh" of the crowd. This Independence Day, celebrate your freedom to avoid this ritual with one of the strategies outlined below.

Pledge Allegiance to Some Other Flag

Join a fringe separatist group calling for an independent Puerto Rico, a Kingdom of Hawaii, or "Operation Mulligan: The

Confederacy Gets a Do-Over." You'll get on a lot of mailing lists, but no one will expect you to celebrate national holidays of your "imperial overlords." In the unlikely event that your group achieves its goals and separates peacefully from the United States, you'll have a new Independence Day to avoid, but cross that bridge when you get to it.

Go to Canada

It worked for generations of draft dodgers, and it will work for you. As the date approaches, slip north across the imaginary line that divides "ninth grade" from "grade nine" and money with men on it to money with a woman on it. You'll have to make this crossing on July 2nd or 3rd, since Canada Day is July 1st. A bunch of liquored-up Americans shooting guns into the air and pushing over cars is alarming enough, but a bunch of liquored-up Canadians doing the same things in an orderly, single-file line is intensely disturbing.

Streak the Lions Club Patriotic Tableau

A bare scrotum flapping in the breeze is an infinitely more vivid and memorable depiction of freedom than Betsy Ross with an embroidery hoop.

Misanthrope-Proposed Constitutional Amendments:

- #28, banning any public activity involving gentle swaying
- #35, mandating an emergency supply of Valium in all public buildings
- #47, clarifying that the right to privacy means that no Misanthrope has to make chitchat in the elevator, on the bus, or with cashiers

American Roulette: Election Day

Every country has that one "thing" that makes their representative identifiable in animated renditions of the United Nations. Spain has bullfighters, India has snake charmers, Ireland has a terrible drinking problem that's ruined its relationship with its children, and so on. America has two: our "If I'm going down I'm taking you all with me" nuclear arsenal, and the once-every-four-years elephant-and-pony show that determines who has access to the big red button. The Misanthrope is not well suited to life in a democracy. Just look at the terminology: party, caucus, convention—even "congress" means "coming together." While few Misanthropes are political animals, some do enjoy voting (those little booths are wonderfully private) and nearly all enjoy taking a three-hour lunch break because "the lines at the polls were so long." The actual facts of Election Day are tolerable, but it can be hard to handle the general hubbub and enthusiasm . . .

Throw Your Vote Away

This works best in years like 2000 and 2004, which saw very emotionally charged elections that essentially ended in ties. People loved talking about these elections, but there was one way to shush talkers from both sides of the aisle: "Well, this mess isn't my fault. I voted for *Ralph Nader.* Wasn't crazy about him, but he was the closest thing to a Dixiecrat on the ballot."

Theme-Party System

Choose a partner. (I understand your suspicions, but trust me, this is worth it.) Assign yourselves each to a party, and as the returns roll in take a shot for each state your party wins. If you set this up in advance, it will add a certain zest to your "get out the vote" canvassing efforts: "Listen. I don't personally care if gay people get state-funded abortions from immigrants, but if I can swing Missouri to the Republicans, I'm gonna get t-t-t-*toasted* on Tuesday, so can we count on your vote?"

Confuse the Poll Workers

"I'm sorry, I just don't know. Can you give me a hint? Well, what if I get the President wrong but I do really well on the extra credit portion with all the senators and bond initiatives and all? Can I still pass? If I fail, do I have to go to Cuba or can I just repeat the administration?"

The Misanthrope's Voting Record:

- 1964: Barry Goldwater
- 1968: Barry Goldwater (write-in)
- 1972: Barry Goldwater (write-in)
- 1976: Barry Goldwater (write-in)
- 1980: Barry Goldwater (write-in)
- 1984: Walter Mondale, because of a lost bet
- 1988: Barry Goldwater (write-in)
- 1992: Barry Goldwater (write-in)
- 1996: Barry Goldwater (write-in)
- 2000: Barry Goldwater (write-in)
- 2004: John Kerry, because too drunk to write in "Barry Goldwater"
- 2008: Stayed home and played StarCraft

Chapter 7

A SMILE MAY OPEN DOORS, BUT A "DO NOT DISTURB" SIGN WILL KEEP THEM SHUT

{ The Vacationing Misanthrope }

Travel is important. You can meet new people (who annoy you as much as the old), try new things (which are remarkably unpleasant), and see the wonders of the world (all of which are surrounded by mosquitoes and beggars). According to public television travel demigod Rick Steves, it's when your luggage is lost and the water is rising that it gets "fun" and you get "stories." For those of us who don't spend our lives planning to *wow* a church potluck, *Eat, Pray, Love* can quickly turn into *Vomit, Swear, Hate*. Montezuma may get his revenge, but we've got some tricks of our own.

"Yes, very colorful. Now may I have my room key?": Getting Things Done in a Siesta Country

Centuries ago, the mighty Spanish Empire circled the globe, bringing Roman Catholicism, the poetic Spanish language, and smallpox to the remotest corners of the globe. Although the colonies have been lost and Spain is now the poor man's France, this legacy is preserved in the widespread custom of the siesta, the obligatory mid-afternoon nap that shuts down every Mediterranean and Latin American country daily, just as a Misanthrope needs to get something done. It's not easy, but the determined Misanthrope can make the best of even a nationwide group activity.

Do It Yourself While Fulfilling "Last Man On Earth" Fantasy

Don't act like you haven't thought about this before—this may be your best chance to experience a world without people. Enjoy the uncrowded streets and the opportunity to refer to the native ham-based dessert as "el crap" without being overheard. If you badly need to take care of a piece of business, you can probably creep into the appropriate office quietly and do it yourself—if someone notices you, just say, "Shh! Siesta!" With any luck, they'll curl up and drop right back off to sleep, leaving you free to work.

Despiertan! Despiertan!

If *you* had a guest, would *you* just flop down for a nap without making sure he was taken care of? No! It's rude if one person does it, and it's rude if all of Paraguay does it. Wake them up. Tech-savvy Misanthropes may be able to hack into the city warning systems and set off the air raid sirens, but the rest of us can simply take a pass through a parking lot, setting off car alarms. If you'd rather localize the disturbance to the person whose help you need, simply drop something large and shattery near their sleeping form. "Oh, did I wake you? I'm *so* sorry, but while you're up . . ." Then once you get what you need, croon a gentle lullaby to coax the clerk back to sleep and tiptoe away before he offers you a margarita.

When in Rome . . .

Even a stopped clock is right twice a day, and it's just possible that these shiftless, equatorial Jimmy Buffetts are onto something.

An excuse to be alone, quiet, with the door locked, in the middle of the day? Enjoy it while you have it.

SIESTA IN A GLASS:

2 measures light rum, 2 measures dark rum, 2 measures gold tequila, 2 measures silver tequila, pineapple juice, grenadine, grain alcohol to taste. Mix all ingredients in a large water glass, then use it to wash down a Valium. Serves one.

Taste It First; *Then* I'll Tell You: What to Do If You're Asked to Try the Horrifying Local Specialty

As a Misanthrope, you're willing to step out of your comfort zone, but only if you don't go past the end of your block. You love trying new brands of nonstick cookware and are always on the lookout for new sarcastic comebacks in case your mother calls again to ask if you're still going to the gym, but that's about as adventurous as you get. Vacation, however, is a time when you're expected to step out of your comfort zone, embrace new cultures, and put things in your mouth that you would normally be too afraid to swat with the back of a John Grisham novel. The zaniest regional dish you've ever tried was the McLobster Rolls at the McDonald's on Cape Cod and you had the McRuns for McEver. When you don't want to come off like an unadventurous Ugly American, but *really* don't want to eat pan-fried yak thyroid sprinkled with caramelized walking sticks, serve up one of these.

It'll Make You Homesick

Because nobody makes pan-fried yak thyroid sprinkled with caramelized walking sticks like good ole mom. "I swear I can taste cumin in there somewhere, but she refuses to give out the recipe."

You Can't Because You're Pregnant

Have you ever seen the absurdly long list of things pregnant women are supposed to avoid? No? Good, neither has Xiu Pak. Assume any uncooked part of a burrowing animal is on there next to cigarettes and a pitcher of Old Fashioneds and send it back to the kitchen.

"Ugh, I Feel *Soooo* Fat You Guys"

Everyone has that one friend who puts on an OBIE-nominated production of letting you know that she's not going to eat any of the spinach and artichoke dip because she's gained weight and feels disgusting. Five minutes of watching her push a carrot stick around the ramekin and whine about not having the discipline for an eating disorder and you wish you had never proposed going out for a Girl's Dinner at all. Take a page from her script, let out a whiny "I could *barely* zip up my pants this morning," and watch the waiters roll their eyes all the way back to the kitchen, signature dish in tow.

OTHER THINGS PREGNANT WOMEN "CAN'T" DO:

Take a sunrise hike, spend a night in a traditional village, listen to a passive-aggressive cab driver talk about how America ruined his country, share a bed

Embrace Your Nationality

The world's opinion of Americans can't get that much worse—do you really think the UN is going to breakup if a few Italians find out you have a uterus the size of a small ham with a lining thicker than castle walls? Be proud of whatever unsavory toiletry you need and ask the pharmacist to get it for you with the gusto of a ship full of immigrants asking Lady Liberty for a new life in the New World.

Involve the Foreign Service

Go to the American Embassy, walk up to a sturdy-looking female agent, show her your passport and empty bag of Tampax Super Plus *Plus* Plus, and say, "I *know* you know, sister."

> **IF THE HOTEL IS OUT OF TOWELS AND YOU JUST CAN'T BRING YOURSELF TO GO TO THE *FARMACIA*:**
> Wad a few pages from the Milan phonebook, a Florence University sweatshirt, cibatta, a bed sheet you cut up with a nail file, your money belt, nothing, just hang out in the bathtub for five days reading Italian *Glamour*

What to Do If Your Travel Partner Is Driving You Crazy

Travel is the only activity besides sex and bridge that Misanthropes are willing to do with a partner. Although Misanthropes savor solitude like a good port, traveling in pairs has its advantages:

1. Navigating a foreign subway system is easier with two sets of eyes on the map instead of one

What's Hindi for Douche?: Buying Embarrassing Products Abroad

Disposable enemas, pregnancy tests, and vaginal cream may not be the most glamorous of drug store items (they don't hold a candle to a ninety-nine-cent copy of *Men In Black II* on VHS at the bottom of the dollar bin), but they're necessary items nonetheless. Even the most stoic Misanthrope gets backed up every now and then, skips a period, and has an itch that just can't be scratched (hopefully not in the same day) and has to take an embarrassing trip to the drug store for some relief. Misanthropes have let minor urinary tract infections turn into full-blown kidney failure to avoid walking the 20 feet from aisle six to the cash register with a box of urinary health supplements and jug of cranberry juice in hand. As people who generally think we're too good for everything and everyone everywhere, it's a painful lift of the snark-colored-glasses when we have to admit publically that we too get gassy, have pubic hair, need more fiber, and sometimes don't feel so fresh . . . *down there*. If you can barely bring yourself to buy industrial absorbency menstrual pads in America from a chain drugstore with big help-yourself-aisles and self-checkouts, what the hell are you going to do when you have to pantomime opening flood gates and babies equal no-no to the *Signor* behind the pharmacy counter in Tuscany?

Bribe Your Travel Buddy to Do It for You

He needs three more Euros to afford that coliseum snow globe and you need to stop using hotel towels as sanitary napkins. Time to make a deal.

2. Splitting meals will make that fifty bucks from grandma last considerably longer

3. Falling asleep on trains is less of a death wish if someone's there to keep an eye on Kyrill, the one-eyed Ukrainian in the seat across from you

4. It's just nice not to be the only person in the car when you're the asshole blocking two lanes of traffic because you can't figure out how to say, "just go around!" in Quebecois.

But for all of their perks, no amount of Mary and Rhoda-style hijinks can save your travel partner from turning into just another shapeless asshole having a fever sweat all over their industrial grade hostel sheets. When your sidekick starts making you wish you'd celebrated finishing your dissertation with an afternoon at Dave & Buster's instead of a swing through the Orient, here's what to do.

Divide and Conquer

"You know—and I'm just spit-balling here—I'd bet we could see twice the countries in half the time if we split up and reunite back in the States. I know you were looking forward to bonding, but the shortest distance between two friends really is a hearty laugh and a shared Flickr account."

Sell Him

The black market only *seems* shady. When you meet Mr. X in the basement of his Korean barbeque joint and make the switch (don't forget to get Travel Buddy good and hooked on heroin *before* you make the trade, or they won't reimburse you for gas), you'll see that he's a real sweetheart and probably wanted to know if Buddy ever had mono or an appendectomy because . . . oh, no reason. I'm just making conversation.

Kill Him
Don't worry—Hungary has got a backlog of DNA to process.

> **AMUSINGLY EUROPEAN PLACES TO HIDE FROM YOUR TRAVEL PARTNER ABROAD:**
>
> In a Beefeater uniform, in a windmill, under the Pope's skirt, behind an Alp, in a fjord, behind the lush, full beard of a Lithuanian woman, in a Nutella crepe

Using Up All Your Accrued Sick Days: What to Do If You're Held Hostage in a Group Abroad

Well, there's a fine how-do-you-do. No sooner did you land in this "undiscovered Middle Eastern oasis" full of "friendly locals, unspoiled beaches, and stunning colonial architecture" than the Emir's shaky, pro-Western government fell like a chubby girl her first time on ice skates. General Khalbi is now in power, having successfully run on the "Death to the American dogs! Slaughter the blue-eyed infidel!" ticket. Hurrying for the first time in your life, you made it to the embassy—too bad the rebel army beat you there. As they march you and the other refuge-seekers around at gunpoint and reinforce the doors and windows, it occurs to you that you might be here for a while. You can handle the guns and the screaming men wielding them; the tricky part will be handling your whiny fellow hostages.

Stockholm Isn't Just a City in Sweden

If the entire Soviet Union can change sides partway through World War II surely one Misanthrope can do it three hours into a hostage situation. Unbutton your top button, figure out how to say, "I've always been aroused by power" in the local dialect of Arabic, and offer to guard the other prisoners while your captors have their evening game of canasta. You'll be one of the boys before you can say "Patty Hearst."

Pretend to Be Mute and Only Able to Read Finnish

It's an elaborate charade, but the effort of keeping it up will be more entertaining than leafing through the three-year-old issues of *People* someone found in the ladies' room. Shrug good-naturedly, draw a little map of Europe on a scrap of paper, and point back and forth between Finland and yourself. If it turns out one of your fellow hostages is an actual Finn, go ahead and learn the language. It's cheaper than Berlitz, and Rosetta Stone doesn't teach you how to say, "If I don't get out of this and you do, you can have my wife."

Make Your Own Soap Opera

You'd never do something this gossipy under normal circumstances, but the situation is dire. Spread a few lies, tell a few tales, and *Dangerous Liaisons* the shit out of your little community. Soon, they'll uncover your little web of deceit and vow never to speak to you again. Problem solved.

Meet a Few of Your Fellow Hostages:

- Bette, a backpacker whose hope of meeting "the real people" has been realized

- Nan, who enjoys reminding her husband Mort that she wanted to go to the Catskills, but no, someone needed to have an "adventure"
- Lucas, a Peace Corps volunteer who thinks this is all George W. Bush's fault
- Arthur, a correspondent for the AP who pretends to understand the political situation

No Refunds on Inner Peace: You've Accidentally Booked a Room at a Meditation Retreat

In retrospect, the English translation on the brochure did seem a little shaky. To your mind, "Our staff ensure The Peace and The Quiet as your cares drift away" meant that a burly gatekeeper kept out the beggars, and that the only person you would see during your week's stay at Infinite Lotus Retreat Gardens would be a quiet waiter you would know only as "Would sir care for another bucket of Tsingtao?" Alas, no. This country was a communist dictatorship for decades and a divine-right monarchy for millennia before that. They're not going to *let* you have a relaxing time, they're going to *make* you. You've accidentally signed up for a week of intensive guided meditation, and the staff has taken your keys and passport "for safekeeping." There's no American embassy on the astral plane, so you'll have to do something in this world.

Sabotage

Throwing an outright tantrum, however tempting, won't work here. If you throw yourself on the floor and scream, they'll just serve you tea or make soothing sounds with singing bowls until you expend all your energy and wind up far more tractable than before. Have your hissy fit not in ways that keep the others at the ashram from concentrating, but in ways that jar them severely once they *are* concentrating. Wait until the meditation room is perfectly still, then sing a few bars of "Louie, Louie." Wait another hour, then produce a mighty fart. If you can keep knocking everyone off their metaphysical perches just as they settle in, you'll be asked to leave before you ruin the chi.

Ninja Misanthrope

Refuse to accept that kung fu movies are fictional, and keep asking the instructors when your ninja powers are going to manifest themselves. In most cases, this will annoy them enough that they let you leave, but one time in a thousand they might cave and teach you something incredibly cool. A Misanthrope may never need to break a man's neck with his ear, but he should know how.

Build a Better Misanthrope

How many times during staff meetings, weekday commutes, or your mother's four-hour "just checking in" phone calls have you wished you could leave your body, browse around Ethan Allen in your spirit form for a while, and come back when it was over? Accept this meditation boot camp as a blessing in disguise and learn skills that will come in handy every day.

Master Chuck, the Berkeley-educated leader of the meditation retreat, has a graying ponytail and thinks kung fu movies perpetuate negative stereotypes. Tran, the college student helping at the front desk, likes kung fu movies and thinks Chuck is boring but has good weed.

Gypsies, Tramps, and Thieves: How to Neutralize Assorted Beggars

When traveling abroad, you begin to realize how very lucky we Americans are. Not because of our political freedoms, our wealth, or our safety, but because our urban poor are amazingly meek compared to those in other parts of the world. Many of ours are silent, relying on the "Will Work for Pot" sign they made out of an empty Trix box to charm passersby out of a few cents. Even the ones who talk generally ask for money instead of following you or telling a long story about How This All Happened: Like the Cutco salesman, they know within five seconds if they've made a sale, and if not they're moving on. This is not the case in other parts of the world. The minute the poor of Delhi see a pointed Anglo-Saxon nose stuck in a copy of *Lonely Planet: India and Some Little Countries That Don't Merit Their Own Book*, they are upon you, relying on persistence and white guilt to drain you of your last rupee. You won't win many friends, but it is possible to enjoy your trip without microfinancing everyone you meet.

Camouflage

Dress in dirty, tattered rags yourself. You'll have to have a few words with the concierge, but better a frosty, "Really, Mr. Turner-Neal, this is a respectable establishment," than ten thousand repetitions of "sir, please, sir, sir!"

Admit Why You're Traveling

Foreigners are just Americans with less money and weird clothes. You didn't come to India to meet people—you've never done anything to meet people. You came here to have some bitchin' goat korma, see some old buildings, and sweet-talk a high-caste cutie into letting you play Hide the Weasel long enough that you can color in India on your "Around the World with Chris's Penis" map. You're a Misanthrope, not Suzanne Somers with a special message from Save the Children. Hire a limousine with a cowcatcher and a big, mean driver named Rabul and see the world the rich bitch way.

Loonies

Distribute Canadian nickels. You'll have to hoof it once they figure it out, but it's funny.

Issues that Have Arisen with the "Around the World with Chris's Penis" Map:

- Yugoslavia broke into several countries, and he has no idea where Tatjana wound up.
- He was pretty drunk with Carmen and had to sketch in a new South American country called "Somewhere in This General Area."
- Sub-Saharan Africa is a big ol' empty patch of scared-of-AIDS white.
- All the girls he's ever met from Australia have been bitches like no one would believe.
- Shit keeps getting independent.

Out Both Ends Like a Dyslexic Fire Hydrant: When You Get Sick Abroad

You don't know where you are, who you are, or what language this newspaper is in. All you remember is that you're far from home, you ate some fish at some point, and that through the curse of some furious island demon you have somehow been in your hotel room vomiting and suffering from diarrhea since before the dawn of time. Suns flared into life, burned for millennia, and were extinguished; the galaxies spun in their lazy dance across the void; and through all these countless eons you've been poised above a squat toilet left over from the French colonists and crying, among other things: Will it ever end?

Imagine the Parasites Are Personal Trainers Working from the Inside

Misanthropes have to maintain a certain level of attractiveness, or people will just assume they're bitter because of their looks. This is the most brutal, painful, and degrading diet you could ever be on, which is why it's working so well. Let the disease run its course, give yourself a day to recover, then go back to that restaurant and ask for seconds. You'll come home wonderfully svelte, and you didn't want to see the new Native Heritage Museum anyway.

Go Ahead and Die

It was going to happen anyway, and at least this way you'll have a pleasantly weird obituary. Also, being buried in a potter's field on an island most people have never heard of is an excellent way to avoid having someone sing "Danny Boy" at your funeral.

How Hemingway Would Have Written If He'd Gotten on Lexapro

Drag yourself to whatever passes for a hospital around here. Fall in love with the beautiful native nurse who cares for you during the weeks of delirium and fever, and during your long recovery win her heart with the countless small kindnesses that prove your unconditional love. Marry her and enjoy a few perfect years together before having the first of your many children, who will grow up with the material advantages of the First World and the stunning natural beauty and laid-back pace of the tropical Pacific. As you spend a contented old age watching sunsets with your beloved wife, still beautiful after all these years, reflect on how pissed your landlord must have been to have had to dispose of your totem pole collection. Gotcha, you old bastard.

Schedule for TV New Caledonia for the Evening You Were the Sickest:

- 7:00 Grainy Australian newscast with shaky vertical hold
- 7:30 Cricket highlights: Tonga vs. Samoa
- 8:00 *Les Simpsons*
- 8:30 It's either a native dance showcase or a human sacrifice, the picture's not good enough to tell
- 9:00 *The Big Lebowski*, dubbed into French, with French subtitles

Cruises: Fuck That Noise

Things that seemed like a good idea at the time: a land invasion of Russia as autumn tints the leaves, marriage to a woman who says "for all intents and purposes," a third *Gilligan's Island* reunion movie without Tina Louise. Things that never seemed like a good idea: a cruise. The next time Shirelle, your still-sexy-at-sixty travel agent, passes you a cruise brochure with the phrase, "Now, I know we said no boats, but this is Nathan Lane's *personal* cruise line, and he performs on *every* voyage. Jessica Walter is opening for him this season, and they do a wonderful little version of 'Friendship' to close the show," show her this page.

No Real Destination

If you take one thing away from this book, let it be this: Misanthropes hate doing something if there's no apparent reason for it. The Misanthrope's oft repeated battle cry, "But why should I, dammit?" gets him kicked out of junior field hockey, Dartmouth, the Sons of the Confederacy, and any other organization that prizes order and no-whining compliance. For a Misanthrope, there is something deeply, intrinsically stupid about taking a boat out into the Gulf of Mexico, going for a few lazy loops, stopping in Charlotte Amalie for half an hour so everyone can get a picture and a puka shell necklace, and then going home. You don't go anywhere; you don't do anything. It just sort of happens to you as you sit there, much like the aging process.

Cabin Fever

Most cruise lines base their rates on a merry little system called "per person double occupancy," meaning that you share a room. What's that? It's just you going? Well, then, spin the devil's roulette wheel to see which other single traveler you'll be paired up with! Looks like you'll be bunking this week with Horny Gaston, a ragin' Cajun fifty-six years young who wants to know "Where you'll be a-sleepin' if'n I pulls me a live one at the Twilight Champagne Dance on the Lido deck tonight."

Buffets

I'm sorry; Ronald Reagan didn't win the Cold War and crush international communism so Americans could wait in line for food while on vacation in their own territorial waters. Win one for the Gipper and go someplace that hires wait staff.

Organized Activities

"You might enjoy on water what you refuse to do on land" didn't work when Christopher Columbus tried to talk his first mate into experimenting a little, and it's not going to get a Misanthrope to enter the limbo contest. Preach.

> ### HORNY GASTON'S GO-TO PICKUP LINE:
>
> "If you was a mudbug, I'd sauté you in a little butter and just eat you right up!"

Chapter 8

I'M NOT AGORAPHOBIC, I JUST DON'T LIKE YOU

{ The Misanthrope about Town }

I believe Shakespeare once said, "Seems like you can't swing a dead cat without hittin' an asshole." Truer words were never spoken, sir. Whether it's a child-heavy Razor scooter on a kamikaze trajectory to your groin or urban peasants trying to raise enough "bread" to make this the best Bonnaroo ever, there are people outside. And every single one of them is *thirsty* for interaction. Unfortunately ObamaCare doesn't cover plastic containment bubbles for people with healthy immune systems and have you seen those homesteader chicks? Arms like thighs! If you *have* to go out to get this week's Swanson Hungry-Man meals and Parrot Bay, here are some tips to get back to your bubble relatively unscathed.

"Oh, my God, Remember Mrs. Beagle?!": What to Do When You Run Into Someone from High School

Absence makes the heart grow fonder, the old saw goes. In some cases, absence makes the heart openly hallucinate, as when the girl you sat behind in tenth-grade algebra and haven't seen since Kurt Cobain was alive spots you, screams your name, and rockets toward you across a crowded PetSmart, knocking over stacked bags of pine shavings in her eagerness to catch up. She was a nice girl, presumably—you can't actually remember, but a smile that big takes practice—but she's become a terrifying adult. Before you can even take a step, she's locked you in a lung-collapsing hug, held you at arm's length ("Just look at you!"), and squeezed you again. It's probably not your fault, but she's giving you hives . . .

Ignorance Is Bliss, Gentle

"Sorry to fart on this impromptu reunion, but I don't remember you at all. It's nothing personal. I took a nasty spill on my board and cracked my head open. My buddy totally got a picture of my brain, and they had to put a steel plate in—you know, 'cause my skull was there on the ground next to me. Anyshit, I don't remember a thing from before college. Not even my name. I call myself Awesome von Pantydrop now."

Ignorance Is Bliss, Harsh

"Sorry to fart on this impromptu reunion, but I don't remember you at all. I guess you're just one of those people who doesn't really stick in the mind, you know? You better run home before your children become attached to the toaster in the absence of a strong maternal figure. You don't want them sticking slices of bread in their mouths and then trying to figure out how to plug themselves in. That kind of thing can sink a custody suit."

True and Steadfast

"Oh, you're so, so kind. No one from high school will even speak to me since the trial, even though I was acquitted of most of the charges! All I'm saying is, if they decide it's wrong to make toddlers fight and allow betting on it, they need to pass a law, am I right? They'd have had nothing on me if I hadn't given the kids meth to put 'em in the fighting spirit. That's industry standard! It's okay to do it to dogs and roosters, but suddenly *children* are *special*. Glad to know I can count on your support."

PLACES YOU *ALWAYS* SEE PEOPLE FROM HIGH SCHOOL:

Supermarket (but only if you haven't showered and are getting a pregnancy test), nickel beer night at the Rusty Nail, Starbucks (not coffee houses in general, just Starbucks), at the Free Clinic (you're the patient; they're the nurse on rotation), anywhere you happen to be vomiting

---

Dinner and a Show: Inappropriately Intimate Conversations in Public

Riddle me this: On a scale of one to ten, how much do you think a Misanthrope cares about a stranger's struggle with ulcerative colitis? If you answered "negative infinity" or "I never pass up a shot at a poop joke," you pass; otherwise, go back to the Introduction to this book and review. The Misanthrope is naturally reluctant to discuss private details—since "I'm so sorry" and "I'm so happy for you" are both traditionally punctuated by hugs, neutrality and avoidance are the only routes open to the Misanthrope, and guess which one sounds better? While the Misanthrope's friends and acquaintances are easily trained not to "open up" unless it's absolutely necessary, the rise of cell phones and the general low-class-ification of American manners ensure that the Misanthrope is always at risk of hearing terrible personal details about strangers.

While you can't cure anyone's irritable bowel syndrome, you can protect yourself against hearing about it.

Pavlov's Dog

Carry an air horn around at all times. Whenever someone near you gets on their cell phone and starts talking about their symptoms, blast the horn. If they turn to you and haughtily say, "Do you mind?" shrug and say, "Edited for content. Not my call." Repeat as necessary until people learn some fucking *reticence*.

Anything You Can Do, I Can Do Better

Sometimes, you can beat 'em by joining 'em. The next time you're dining out and patrons at an adjoining table start in on edema, mucus, and that *awful* burning feminine itch, pull a chair up to the table and sit down. Match them draining sore for draining sore, -ostomy for -ostomy, dental mishap for dental mishap. The naturally vivid imagination of the Misanthrope, developed over a solitary childhood, will serve you well here.

The Poor Man's *Ally McBeal*

If you can choke back your horror and forget that these are *real* people talking about *real* enemas *real* loud, you can delude yourself into thinking you're actually watching a mid-level prime-time drama-edy. You wouldn't have thought so before you came into this restaurant, but there's apparently a thin line between inexcusable rudeness and regional dinner theater. So sit back, pretend the lighting is marginally better, and try to enjoy the show.

> **Original Cast of the Outback Steakhouse Production of *The Poor Man's Ally McBeal*:**

- Starring Katey Sagal as "Woman Who Doesn't Know What She's Going to Do with Teenage Daughter"
- Laurie Metcalf as "Woman Who Thinks the Daughter Should Just Be Sent to Live With Her Father"
- David Boreanaz as "Guy Who Believes in Second Chances"
- A special cameo by Jessica Walter as "I Heard About Your Daughter and I Want You to Know You're Both in My Prayers"

Today on *Sally*: Over-Attentive Salespeople and the Misanthropes Who Hate Them

Misanthropes like to shop with the cool, efficient precision of a Mossad assassination: Get in, take care of business, and get out before anyone starts asking questions. By contrast, marketing and sales executives like to imagine their stores as an eternal first day of college, full of smiling teenagers sidling up and being aggressively friendly. These "professional greeters" pop out questions like a cobra spitting venom—"Hi! How are you doing today? Can I help you find anything? Have you shopped at Jeans A-Go-Go before?! Would you like to sign up for our mailing list!? Gooble-gobble, one of us!" It's not their fault—they've been indoctrinated, and were probably blank slates to begin with—but that doesn't mean you have to play along.

"Ani Soneh et Kulam" (Your Hebrew Phrase for the Day Is "I Hate Everyone!")

Learn six or seven words of Lao, Hebrew, or any language exotic enough that you're willing to bet the salesperson won't recognize it. Repeat it with different inflections in response to everything the salesperson says. Be sure you don't choose a language that sounds like anything commonly taught in public schools, or you'll have to deal with *"Puedo helparte con los jeans. Los. Jeans. Es muy 'relaxed fit.' Por el mucho grande."*

Secret Shopper

Misanthropes aren't famed for making others happy, but sometimes doing so can work to your advantage. As soon as the salesperson runs through their "Hihowareya . . ." spiel, smile and take their hands. (I know it's an effort. Trust me.) "I'm from the Central Office," you'll say. "You're the best greeter in all of Zone One . . . hell, in all of Area Three! You're destined for amazing things, kiddo. I have to go check the store layout now—you stay here and keep up the good work! You'll be hearing from me soon." The jury's still out on whether creating false hope counts as a good deed for community service purposes, but this strategy should buy you enough time to snag a few practical button-downs.

The Electric Slide

Just taze 'em. It's not classy, it's not elegant, and it's not "technically legal," but a few dozen volts to the neck shuts people up faster than a duct-tape facial. The salesperson will think they just got lightheaded from their single-minded determination to "provide excellent, consumer-driven customer service solutions," and no one else will notice a greeter with a blanker-than-usual gaze.

WORST-CASE SCENARIO:

If they will not leave you alone, you may have to do all your shopping at the corner drugstore. It may mean surviving on a diet of peppermint candies and wild cherry seltzer, and wearing only beach coverups all year round, but at least no one at Walgreen's cares if you're having a good day. They can tell by your diet that you're not.

"I Already Give to Ron Paul": What to Do When You're Approached by a Charity Street Canvasser

For a group of people who jump at the opportunity to help the dispossessed, disadvantaged, and disenfranchised for $8.95 an hour in a non-court ordered capacity, Charity Street Canvassers are some straight-up assholes. It's not that you don't *want* to help; it's just that you . . . well, no, sorry; it is that you don't want to help. You feel for the dolphins, teen moms, and transgendered postal workers of the world, you really do, but you'd feel for them a lot more if their voice on the street wasn't an overeager summer intern convinced she can change the world with a BA in sociology from Bryn Mawr and a moment of your time. Charity Street Canvassers are everything that the Misanthrope isn't: plucky, outgoing, patient, compassionate, extroverted, and totally willing to wear an over-sized T-shirt and fleece vest in public. As if their mere existence wasn't already enough, they then had to go and station themselves along your route to and from work, making it all but impossible to avoid their cheerful "Good morning, sir! Do you have a minute to talk about [adjective] [mammal] from [impoverished African country or lesser known Canadian territory]'s rights?" at least twice a day.

Instead of mumbling about how sorry, but you're really late for a meeting, or some equally weak cop-out they've been trained to expect, wallop their idealism with one of these zingers.

Hey, Charlize Theron Is African

If she asks you if you have time today for the Impoverished Orphans of Chad, tell her you *are* an Impoverished Orphan of Chad and on behalf of the whole village, you gotta say, she's doing a helluva job.

Hire Her to Canvass for You

You're using an "evening mist-scented" decorative candle as deodorant, there's twelve years of payments left on your student loan, and your boss is going to kill you if he finds out you've been stealing toilet paper from work again—who's to say you're *not* a 501(c)(3) certified charity?

Contact Their Local Draft Officer

Ask "Charlie" if he's got a few minutes, *hippie*.

If you can't bring yourself to engage in any kind of verbal interaction with her whatsoever, turn to the strategy that Misanthropes have been using to avoid enemies stopped in their path since time immemorial: Break into a run, cross your fingers, and scream *"No whammies! No whammies! No whammies!"* as you fly down the street.

Human Speed Bumps: Getting Around a Gaggle of "Mall Walkers"

Misanthropes are invariably always running late—they have no interest in taking slow, romantic strolls through the city, stopping only occasionally to shake off a June bug from their parasol and tell the good old boy on their arm to keep talking because a girl could get used to sweet words like that. No, mostly they just power walk and tell people to get the fuck out of their way. But when three city blocks, two minutes, and a quick jog in moderately comfortable nude pumps is all that stands between the Misanthrope and breezing through the office door on time, fellow pedestrians become obstacles and none slow you down more than a group of "Mall Walkers." You may not know what Mall Walkers are, but trust me, they live to annoy. Mall Walkers are a group of three or more people who walk side-by-side at an annoyingly slow pace, thereby taking up the entire width of the sidewalk and forcing everyone behind them to match their snail's pace.

Red Rover, Red Rover, Send Misanthrope Over

Get a good running start and hurl yourself at the weak point of their chain. Technically, if you break through you're supposed to return the challenge to them, but you're late for work and that bagel in your messenger bag isn't going to eat itself.

Also They Might Get a Blister

Little brothers may be total dicks, but every now and then they come to the table with some good ideas. Sync your walking so every time you take a step forward you step on the back of a Mall Walker's shoe, causing her to partly un-shoe herself and trip. The trio will quickly get the hint, temporarily dismantle, and let you walk by—or get all whiny and threaten to tell on you.

Throw Yourself Into Oncoming Traffic to Prove a Point

It's a little extreme and Blue Cross Blue Shield might cancel your policy for claiming another invaluable teaching moment-related hospital visit, but like most agents of social change, you gotta take some risks.

OTHER REASONS WHY YOU'RE LATE:

Eating another bowl of Kashi, got involved in an intense cuddle session with your cat and didn't want to be rude, you had to see how your Keno numbers did, you realized your shirt was ambiguously see through, you had the weirdest craving to hear the theme song for *Maude* and it took forever to download

A True Man Pisses Alone: Crossing Swords at the Urinal

Women expect certain things from men, but these expectations change over time. The cave woman expected her man to bring home slabs of raw mammoth from time to time, and to occasionally impregnate her with a sturdy child—while the ladies of the Roman Empire expected their men to win glory in battle. A woman who hit her prime in the 1950s wanted a man who was a good provider, while the hipster chick of today hopes for a fellow lurid with ironic tattoos, and sporting a PBR gut barely contained by an Iron and Wine T-shirt. By contrast, men have always expected the same things from other men: A tacit agreement that women are irrational, that emotional displays be confined to sports contexts, and that in the men's room one neither chats nor takes a urinal next to one already in use. It seems so simple, yet all men have had the appalling experience of standing at the pisser, hose in hand, calmly making room for more beer, and having a total stranger sidle up to the next-door unit and ask you if you think the Oilers have what it takes this year. This is not okay, as he will soon discover.

Waterfall
Reach over and hit the flush lever on his urinal as hard as you can. If the building is old enough to have pre low-flow plumbing, the spray resulting from the powerful cascade will wet the front of his pants with a mixture of water, urine, and deodorizing cake.

Cruise Fail
It used to mean only one thing when one man approached another in the men's room and started talking: "Listen, no offense, but you're not really what I'm looking for right now. I'm in the mood for someone a little younger, sort of a confused and experimenting vibe. I'm a little tired of waiting, though . . . ah, what the hell. Just bend over the sink and pretend you've never done this before."

Look Directly at His Penis
Even men who ignore the other rules never break the "don't glance over" rule, but he started it. Gaze evenly at his member. Many men can't go with someone watching, and even those who can still feel pretty damn awkward.

> ### I FEEL PRETTY:
>
> Another major lapse in men's room etiquette is the extended grooming session in the mirror. A quick neatening is fine, even desirable, but some men (Europeans) will stand there for fifteen minutes, smoothing, straightening, checking, arranging, plucking, what have you. The next time you're confronted with this, pull out a safety razor and start shaving your underarms. He'll leave.

I Find the Defendant Sexy: Getting Out of Jury Duty

Being an American citizen carries with it certain duties. Some of these are fun, like reporting suspected communists to the House Un-American Activities Committee; some are heavy, heavy crosses, like jury duty. A Misanthrope might enjoy watching the defendant squirm like a worm on a hook as the bailiffs bring out the bloody overcoat, the skulls, and the videotaped confession he put in the wrong envelope and mailed to *American Idol* in place of his upbeat rendition of "At Last." The jury room is what daunts the Misanthrope: Being locked in with eleven of his peers, listening as they talk on and on about how the evidence made them *feel*? The law can compel to attend the jury selection, but there's no penalty for being way, way too ape shit to be chosen. Here are some sample answers to common *voir dire* questions that will have the lawyers shouting "Challenge!"

Q: If the case and the law required it, would you have a problem assigning the death penalty?

A: Not at all, I don't think we use it nearly enough. I'll tell you how we should keep America beautiful—send more litterbugs to the death house. They'll have a hard time throwing their cigarette butts on the ground with 20,000 volts flying through their bodies. Am I right?

Q: From the media coverage of the case, have you formed an inflexible opinion regarding the defendant's guilt or innocence?

A: Not from the media, but those beady little eyes look like a killer's to me. Not that I blame him, though. The victim does come across as a bitch.

Q: Do you have any prior relationship with the defendant, the judge, any of the other potential jurors, or any counsel present?

A: No, but I wouldn't mind trying something with that sassy little court reporter over there. She looks like a fun time.

Q: Have you ever been tried or convicted for a felony?

A: Not in this country. Let me tell you, when they say, "Don't moon the Pope," you better not moon the Pope. You'd think he'd never seen an ass before!

Q: Do you understand the fact that the defendant has been brought to trial is not necessarily an indication of his guilt?

A: Oh, I'm *fully* aware of that. Wink.

TRIVIA:

Jury Duty is the third-most erotically charged Pauly Shore movie, after *Son in Law* and *Bio-Dome*. (Source: Pauly Shore.)

It's a Free Show, But You Get What You Pay For: When the Misanthrope Witnesses a Public Display of Affection

Feathers already ruffled because you had to give up a Saturday afternoon tending to your prize-winning creeping ivy to go to the mall and pick up your nephew from his job at Pacific Sunwear. You sit down in the food court to wait for him and enjoy a handful of teriyaki chicken samplers, when at the next table you see a couple locked in a passionate embrace. Or as passionate as you can be when you're slurping at someone's face like a hog at a trough and your promise ring is caught in his hair. As they grind away at each other like a pimply mortar in a no-head-on-the-first-date pestle, you're disgusted. Not by young love, not by open sexuality, not even by the teriyaki chicken—they're just terribly homely. Your nephew still has a dozen Billabong T-shirts to fold. Time to take action.

Retaliate

It's wholly undignified, but unzip those Jordaches and start furiously masturbating.

Educate

You're a visual person by nature and always thought it would be easier to tell little Jill about the birds and the bees if you could plop her down in front of *Back Door Sluts 9* and give her a play-by-play, instead of wasting twenty minutes trying to think of a way to say "slides it in and out" without vomiting. Well, here's an opportunity to do it your way without dipping into your "special" DVD collection or getting a visit from Child Protective Services!

Meg Ryan's Hair Looked Great

Call over a waiter, point to the couple and say, "I'll have what *they're* having!" Not because it will accomplish anything, really, just because an opportunity to work an iconic Rob Reiner gag into your daily life is genuinely exciting.

Super Eight

"*Get a room!*" No but really. Get them a room. The Dallas-Fort Worth area features a number of clean, affordable motels suitable for the businessperson on the go or the leisure traveler. Many are convenient to downtown shopping and dining, and even offer free Wi-Fi! Enjoy a delicious continental breakfast before strolling out and enjoying what the Metroplex has to offer. (Paid for by Dallas-Fort Worth Chamber of Commerce.)

WHY YOU SHOULD STAY AND PLAY IN DALLAS–FORT WORTH:

The Dallas Cowboy's newly renovated stadium is a sports fan's dream and an architectural delight; for all of your shopping needs, head to the galleria, or for a more leisurely atmosphere, The Shops at Mockingbird Center, the area's rich cultural heritage is represented; several musical theater groups and the award-winning Dallas and Kimbell museums of art; if you're craving something a little more "south of the border," head to El Phoenix for the area's best Mexican food; so y'all come on down, we'd love to see ya!

Chapter 9

IF A MAN'S HOME IS HIS CASTLE, WHY CAN'T I HAVE A MOAT?

{ At Home with the Misanthrope }

Now that you have your Swanson meals and Parrot Bay, you deserve to enjoy them in a little peace and quiet. But as Maya Angelou said as she accepted her honorary doctorate from the University of Mississippi, "Wantin' ain't gettin'. Wish in one hand and crap in the other and see which gets full first."* Scholars believe this was Dr. Angelou's poetic way of saying, you can't always get what you want—in this case a worry-free evening at home—but with a little savvy, you can repel even the worst assaults on your peace of mind.

(*This never happened, but don't you wish it did?)

You've Already Come This Far, Can You Please Just Bring the Pad Thai to My Apartment?: How to Get the Delivery Boy from the Lobby to Your Door

Any Misanthrope worth her weight in cold, detached stares knows that ordering in is always what's for dinner. Not only does it allow you to enjoy cuisines of many lands without, you know, the "people" and "culture," but you also don't have to worry about people whispering because your date is a crossword puzzle. In fact, with more and more restaurants participating in online ordering, your interaction with the outside world is limited to the amount of time it takes you to open the door, trade money for food, and grunt, "thank you." But society will always find a way to make the Misanthrope's life harder, and more times than not, the delivery person calls and insists the Misanthrope come down to pick up her food. This, of course, begs the question: If you were going to leave your apartment to get food, why did you order delivery?

Managed Incoherence

Your phone rings.

Delivery Person: Did you order [fill in the blank with Asian country of your choice] food?

The Misanthrope: Yep.

Delivery Person: Okay, come down and get it; I'm in the lobby.

The Misanthrope: Okay, will do! Just bring it up to [insert your apartment number here, confidently]!

Delivery Person: Oh. Uh. Okay. [Hangs up and, beaten, actually delivers your food]

In the rock/paper/scissors that is human interaction, the paper of nonsense covers the rock of laziness every time.

The Elephant Man Likes Mu Shu Pork, Too!

This may not be the most moral route, but then again where's the morality in being forced to put on pants to retrieve your dinner in the middle of Final Jeopardy? When the delivery person calls and tells you to come downstairs to get your food, claim that you're homebound because of PKK. (The most famous PKK is a Kurdish terrorist group, but who says it can't also be a horribly disfiguring disease?) Then right before you open the door, don a long, heavy, black veil and retrieve your food with a pale, trembling hand. If you do it just right, they may pity you and start throwing in extra egg rolls.

Promise Them a Wonderful Tip. A *Heavenly* Tip

And then when you answer the door and take your food, hand them a copy of *The Watchtower.* When the delivery person asks, "What's this?" respond, with a beatific smile, "It's the best tip you'll ever get." Then close and lock the door.

FORTUNE COOKIE FORTUNES FOR MISANTHROPES:

"You'll be asked to work from home in the near future." "Privacy is the stripes on the tiger of solitude." "You will meet a tall, interesting man. But don't worry, he'll go away soon."

It's Considerably Sexier in Porn: Waiting Around for the Serviceman

Misanthropes aren't really synonymous with "patience." The initial seventeen seconds it takes for your TV to find the satellite signal can fill a Misanthrope with enough rage-bile to create a gallstone the size of a billiard ball, and that only takes seventeen seconds. When something breaks around the house, you're given a twelve-hour window of time in which the serviceman may or may not come, depending on how brutal his Life Drawing teacher's critiques are during this morning's mini-workshop. You've used your Ped Egg, waxed your floors, and changed the air conditioner filter, and it's only been forty-five minutes. When he finally shows up (charcoal smeared and vulnerable), be ready for him.

The Blanche Devereaux

Consider this: A home-service professional/repairman is an excellent person for a Misanthrope to have a fling with. He's on a schedule, if a loose one, so he'll have to get to business and leave soon after the deed is done, and the uniform adds a pleasant element of interchangeability—you're not screwing Dan, a member of the Reno Light and Power Company Family, Who's Here to Help!—you're screwing the meter reader. So as you wait, dress in something that says "attainable" and knock back a couple of gin rickeys. You'll have to be a little drunk to say, "Let's give it a whirl, big boy," to a stranger, but it might be worth it.

The Annie Wilkes

If the Jersey Devil scampered into your split-level ranch home during dinner, clicked his little cloven hooves thrice and wowed you with a rendition of "Simple Gifts" on his fife of hellfire, you wouldn't just marvel how you thought he'd be taller ("Really? *Knee*-high?"), point him to the turnpike, and go back to your chicken parm— you'd make a cage out of the dryer and a combination lock and be the richest insurance adjuster in Trenton. A repairman physically standing in your home is a creature just as mythical and should thus be given the same treatment. Lock him up in the utility closet and pull him out whenever anything needs to be fixed. You'll never have to wait for the cable guy or Orkin man again.

The Title IX

Fix it yourself before he gets there, and say "But nice hustle," before heartily patting him twice square on the bottom.

> ## OTHER THINGS THE JERSEY DEVIL CAN PLAY ON HIS FIFE OF HELLFIRE:
>
> "My Heart Will Go On," "Hot Cross Buns," "In-A-Gadda-Da-Vida," the theme from *Get Smart*, "Love Shack," the Harvard fight song, "Hey Ya," "Wonderwall," "Old Man River," just scales, but he's developing a really good tone

I Have Learned What It Means to Hate with My Entire Body and Soul: That One Thing Your Roommate Does That Makes You So Angry Your Eyes Leak Blood

Misanthropes are used to being annoyed. Like traffic noises in the city, it's our constant background; we'd be worried if it *stopped*. It's a simple truth, learned by rote at Mother's knee: Thirty days hath September, Roy G. Biv, most things are annoying, with liberty and justice for all. We're used to these frustrations, and yet . . . the roommate. He sets a jam-sticky knife down on the counter you *just* wiped. He can't take a shower without playing "Pour Some Sugar on Me" at top volume. *He puts things back in the freezer without resealing them.* And somehow the *Misanthrope* is the crazy one, just because after the thirty-seventh time you found an empty cardboard tube in the toilet paper dispenser, you got a knife from the kitchen drawer and chased him around the apartment trying to get a slice off that "fat little ham hock" of his to brush generously with a honey maple glaze, splash with pineapple juice, bake for fifteen to twenty minutes until golden brown, and serve to his pastor. *Completely* unfair.

Take a Mulligan

When you told your therapist that you were one opened box of freezer burnt pot-stickers away from entering the glamorous world of cannibalism and classic American dinner cuisine, she looked at you as though calculating whether or not you were a danger to yourself or others. You explained in a trembling voice, "No, you don't understand—it's that one . . . *thing* . . . he does . . . that I can't . . . fucking . . . stand." The judgmental light in her eyes instantly extinguished itself as she was transported back to a studio apartment in the '70s, a shared bathroom, and her roommate's wet towel haphazardly thrown on the wooden hamper. "I think it's important that you remember that sometimes it's healthy to get angry." Everyone who's had a roommate knows exactly what you're talking about, so go ahead and kill yours—the jury will totally understand.

Figure Out What *His* "One Thing" Is and Do It

It may go against everything you stand for, but going through a quick phase of humming when you watch TV is worth Fudgesicles that don't faintly taste like trout for the duration of your lease.

Reward Him Every Time He Remembers to Reseal His Frozen Goods

Well look at that! Maybe an old dog can learn new tricks!

Some Famous Murder Victims and Their Infuriating Habits:

- Mr. and Mrs. Borden—endlessly clicked retractable pens
- Sharon Tate—always pronounced library "lie-barrie"
- Sal Mineo—licked his fingers after every meal
- The Black Dahlia—never cleaned the lint trap after doing her laundry
- Yitzhak Rabin—wore short-sleeved shirts with a tie

Dollar-Store Exorcism: What to Do If Your House Is Haunted

You finally got that promotion at work and can afford to buy the old Hicken place on the edge of town. It's the perfect house for a Misanthrope like you:

- It sleeps thirty-two so you'll never have to begrudgingly offer to sleep on the couch when a houseguest conveniently starts complaining about her "bad back."
- There are tons of secret passageways to hide in when your cousin and his girlfriend are in town for the Gathering of the Juggalos and ask if they can stay an extra night.
- There are four levels of creaky floorboards aching for the kind of repair that only someone who's spent a lifetime of Saturdays watching *This Old House* can provide.
- It's permanently shrouded in a cloud of thick mist so the neighbors won't get an eyeful when you don't have the energy to close the blinds as you get ready for bed.
- There was a triple homicide in the living room in 1932 so you know there's crown molding!

The papers are signed, the last truck has been unloaded, and you're ready to enjoy your new home when the lights start flickering, there's a sudden gust of wind, and a deep, raspy voice bellows "*Get . . . out.*" Uh, you didn't take a high interest loan on a multimillion-dollar Isolation Mansion just to end up with a goddamn *ghost* in the house, thank you. Here's how to stand your ground and give Casper the old heave-ho.

Kumbay *Ahhhh*!

The cheapest and easiest thing to do is clean the "negative air" by doing a simple sage stick smudging. Unfortunately veteran ghosts are rarely intimidated by that kind of hippie-dippie-mumbo-jumbo and burning sage smells like straight up hot dogs and cigarettes.

Hire a Professional Ghost Hunter to Detect for Any Paranormal Activity

Yeah you already know for sure there's a ghost in your house from all the late night talks about cute boys and absentee fathers, but watching a Wiccan divorcee lurk around your house and take "energy readings" with a coat hanger shoved into car battery is just too good to pass up.

Fall in Love with It

Invest in a small pottery wheel and . . . 'eh, never mind. He just left her in the end anyway and you've been hurt too many times.

Haggle

This is getting ridiculous. The walls won't stop bleeding long enough to paint them Harvest Wheat and the little boy trapped in the attic is stuck for eternity in the midst of puberty. If you're not going anywhere but your new supernatural friends won't stop changing the channel every Monday night at eight to *How I Met Your Mother*, the only thing left to do is make a deal: Pipe down or start paying rent. Hey, it worked for your mom when you were in high school.

BOYS THE GHOST THINKS ARE CUTE:

Maulik Pancholy, Nick Jonas, Neil Patrick Harris

A Misanthrope's Best Frenemy: How to Knock Your Cat Down a Peg or Two in a PETA-Friendly Way

All stereotypes are based on some truth. (Or at least that's what your racist grandfather always says when you yell at him for saying that all black people know how to play the trumpet.) The stereotype of a Crazy Old Cat Lady didn't come out of nowhere. When you're too . . . *eccentric* to mix and mingle with mainstream society but still need someone around to listen to you point out plot inconsistencies in *Poirot* episodes, the logical answer is to get a cat. Cats are reasonably quiet and they provide companionship, but also understand that sometimes you both need your space. It's only a matter of time before a Misanthrope thinks it's a good idea to rescue a homeless cat, like a knight in tweed armor. But anybody who's actually ever had a cat knows that just because it's an animal (and yes, an adorable one), it doesn't mean that it won't have the capacity to be a stone-cold bitch when it wants to, as well. Sure, she's asleep in your lap soothing you with her gentle purr one minute, but then she's knocking over your prized Kelsey Grammar statuette the next because you were fifteen minutes late with her evening Tender Vittles. God forbid you actually get a love life and stay out all night or you'll come home the next morning only to find your apartment riddled with cat turds. If the Humane Society won't take her back . . .

Eye for an Eye, Poop for a Poop

Your couch is clawed to hell, there's a thin layer of cat hair on every article of clothing you own, and you've started telling people that the rug is yellow because the hardware store won't sell you industrial-strength carpet cleaning spray anymore because they think you're cooking meth—this bitch needs to be put in her place. Unfortunately the only thing in the apartment that is decidedly hers is the litter box. Pound some fiber, cop a squat over her commode, remind yourself that you used to have *two* antique candle holders, and show her who's boss.

Cut Her Catnip with Oregano

It certainly pisses you off when your dealer does it to you.

Get Your Hardwood Floors Professionally Waxed and Watch Her Go Flying

Make sure to take video so later you can add Wreckx-N-Effect's "Rump Shaker" in the background, upload it to YouTube, and make her an overnight meme sensation.

ULTIMATE REVENGE:

Have your pet spayed or neutered and claim it was for its own good.

Moving: How a Misanthrope Gets Their Shit From Point A to Point B (While Having a Drink at Point C)

Moving has to be one of the most unpleasant things to do in the entire world behind attending a capella concerts and making love. It's always hot and humid the day you have to move, no matter what time of the year it is; trying to figure out in what order all of your oddly shaped furniture should go into the U-Haul so everything fits in one trip is like taking a test for autism; and there's just so much *schlepping*. Most people ease the pain of moving by relying on their friends and family to pitch in and lend a hand, but when you've consistently responded to every friend's e-mail asking the same favor of you with, "Sure, would love to help!" followed by a couple lines of white space and then, "J/K J/K LOL ROFL!!" in 72 point hot-fuchsia comic sans font, they don't typically line up to grab a box. If you have a few hours left on your lease and not a whole lot of options, try any of these on for size.

One Word

Teleportation. It's not real, but it's also not crazy to think it could be someday . . .

Make Friends *Real* Fast

People still use Myspace, right? Sign up for a profile, upload one of those mortifying Glamour Shots your mom made you sit for when you were in Palm Springs visiting your grandparents in 1986, friend every guy within five miles of your zip code who looks like they could actually be from Florida, send out an e-blast that throws around the terms "desperate" and "help" a lot, and sit back while your new friends do all the work.

Light Treason

Go to the army/navy surplus store, buy a military uniform from the branch of your choice (and while you're there, get yourself some fancy decorations and a few badges of honor too—you deserve it), and pretend to be a serviceman so not only will Uncle Sam pay for you to move, he'll do it himself! It's probably going to involve a lot of tedious paperwork and will in no way be as easy as the above makes it sound, if it's possible at all, but at least you got some cool clothes out of it?

Move Six Boxes to the Curb, Get Winded, and Give Up

You got the orienteering badge in Boy Scouts. You know what poison ivy looks like and remember that when the big red line hits the vertical black line, you're heading north or there's six more weeks of winter or something weird. Either way, being homeless can't be *that* hard, right?

MYSPACE PAGE WELCOME SONG:

"I'm Every Woman," Chaka Khan

It's Always on My Poker Night: Who to Send to the Home Owner's Association Meeting as Your Proxy

You appreciate your apartment: It's where you eat, sleep, bathe, relax, diagnose yourself with things you read about on WebMD when you can't sleep—in other words, it's home. But like a girlfriend tweezing her areola hairs in bed next to you while you read the *Times*, sometimes it's really better to leave a little mystery.

You don't need to know *everything* that goes on in your building. You appreciate that Kacho will be replacing the insulation in the boiler room Tuesday afternoon at 3:30 P.M., but unless it interrupts your post-*90210*, pre-*OC* nap, you really don't give a flying fuck what brand insulation he goes with. Those decisions are best left to people who replace the empty void in their lives by joining a meaningless bureaucratic circle jerk rather than relying on alcohol and Twitter like normal people. This is, of course, your Home Owner's Association. And you want nothing to do with the people who signed up. Unfortunately, they've started to complain about how you keep hassling them with questions that were already answered at previous meetings and insist you start doing your "neighborly duty" and join. Be a man, Misanthrope, and send a proxy instead. But who . . . ?

Your Niece

She's competent, gentle, has decent penmanship, and knows when to throw in a good joke. (Not a *great* joke; she always goes the somewhat obvious route, but then again she doesn't workshop her material, but I guess what works for her works for her.) All in all she'd be an adequate proxy—nothing memorable, but efficient nonetheless.

Strap a Tape Recorder to Your Helper Monkey Bartholomew's Back and Send Him in on a Tiny Tricycle While Blasting Toto's "Africa"

Equally as efficient and considerably more memorable.

Send an Edible Arrangement

You'll have no idea if the soda machines in the lobby will continue selling Nestea or switch to Lipton Brisk, but at least you can stay in your apartment listening to the "throwback jamz" station on Pandora and clean out your fridge without your neighbors thinking you're an asshole.

Bartholomew Also Covered Your Ass . . .

- When you needed a ride home from the eye doctor's
- When you really needed another pair of eyes on that draft proposal
- When you had a bad trip and needed to be talked down
- When you *really* wanted ice cream but *really* didn't want to put on makeup
- When you needed a character witness
- When you were drinking too much and someone had to confront you
- That time you had lice and CVS was out of Nix

If You Can't Afford to Fumigate: The Misanthrope's Guide to Tactfully Getting Rid of a Houseguest

Let it speak worlds that houseguests are so bad, it's common for people other than Misanthropes to despise them—*people* people. Like, healthy, levelheaded, All-American, wine-tasting on the weekend, I-jog-before-work-because-it-invigorates-me kind of people. Yeah. It just got real. What makes houseguests so universally loathed is that they're like a thorn in the side of your otherwise comfortable daily routine: They're not necessarily destructive or even *that* painful, but they just sit there in a little pool of inconvenience and make everything harder than it has to be, radiating little waves of dull pain. You can't watch the news as you get ready for work in the morning because they're still asleep. You have to wear a bra around the house or it's your fault for jiggling, not their fault for staring. If they see you in the kitchen making yourself Ramen noodles, you're now making *two* packs of Ramen noodles and are socially obligated to eat the unsettling shrimp flavor. If a Misanthrope opened a bed and breakfast, it would be called The Move Along Now—here's how to live up to the name.

Keep the Thermostat at 60
Because you find it "bracing."

Sell Your Couch on Craigslist
And use the $40 you get to buy a foam puzzle of Frank Lloyd Wright's architectural masterpiece *Fallingwater*.

Start a Post-Punk Jam Band Called Judge Judy & The Sidebars
And practice a lot.

Hoard
Every pizza box and every cocktail napkin is a bulwark against intruders. Don't stop washing out and stacking your margarine tubs until you can't see the floor or walls and one room is completely off limits. If the health department comes and condemns your house, stand on your roof nude and defiant, and go down with the ship.

Become a Buddhist and Renounce Your Worldly Possessions

Maybe they wouldn't stay with you every time they're in Salt Lake if you didn't have Nintendo 64, "full flavor" colas, and a sexy bead curtain.

Highlights from the Stuff the Heath Department Found in Your Stash:

- A solid brick of Panda Express receipts
- Some birds
- A bizarre number of SAT prep books
- A fully customized '89 Gremlin
- A spotted owl habitat
- Part of a Bolivian soccer team and a pile of human bones
- A Torah scroll
- A dozen tubs of muscle-building whey powder
- Cans of tomato paste
- A portal to Narnia

I Was Just Calling to See If You Still Love Me: Managing Passive-Aggressive Voicemails, E-mails, and Texts

Pop quiz: Which of these statements is the most likely to cause the hearer to spontaneously combust?

1. I hate you.
2. I never loved you.
3. I've always hated you.

4. Hi, I know you're mad at me, but I just wanted to tell you goodnight and that I really want to be friends again. So I hope you can forgive me, I feel like I've forgiven you a lot of times, but I understand if you're still mad.

If you chose any of the first three, keep watching light comedies starring Doris Day and Rock Hudson, and give this book to your neighbor with the eight-foot-high barbed wire fence. He'll use it more. Nothing is more infuriating than passive-aggressive behavior, from the simple *Gaslight*-style doublespeak of "I know you think I'm lying" to the oh-poor-me majesty of "You'll wish you'd treated me better when I'm dead." Passive aggression is so elegant and seemingly effortless that it is considered an art in some countries — in Portugal, the best practitioners compete for a generous government stipend. Technology has been an unqualified boon for the passive-aggressive. They used to have to be in the same room as their victims or compose a letter on paper; now, they can send a text message, voicemail, or e-mail the instant a sentiment occurs to them. You'll never eradicate this practice, but you can send it to the spam folder.

Buy Them a One-Way Ticket to Damascus

Passive-aggressive people have seldom undergone actual hardship — if they had, they wouldn't think it was such a big deal if you forgot to return their "what's up" text. Make the scales fall from their eyes. Clean out their checking account, smash their china, and slap them around a little bit. Afterward, patiently explain *that's* what abuse and hardship feel like.

Fight Fire with Fire

Respond to everything they say with "I'm sorry you feel that way." They may get it or they may not, but it'll drive them up the wall.

Boot 'Em

Get a Dog. When they're mad at you, they just shit on the floor, and you can solve that problem with a paper towel and fifteen minutes in the Quiet Crate.

CATARINA SALAZAR'S SUCCESSFUL APPLICATION FOR A PORTUGUESE GOVERNMENTAL PASSIVE-AGGRESSION PRACTITIONER STIPEND:

She has given her daughter sets of progressively smaller bowls each year for her birthday, each time while saying, "These will make it easier for you to eat smaller portions."

He Can't Be *That* Good: When Your Neighbor Has Loud Sex

Despite his reputation for being a sour killjoy, the Misanthrope leads a life full of quiet, exquisite pleasures. The delicate shine of the morning sun on dewy grass. A perfect martini. The click as the deadbolt slides into place on the Friday afternoon before a three-day weekend. These little sensual treasures are all best enjoyed as the Misanthrope likes to live—in perfect, uncorrupted solitude and silence. And the broad across the hall is ruining all of them by cater-wauling like a dying banshee just because she got lucky at last call with some guy named Chase with a "degree" in trick bartending and a blond wedge cut. She's yelling so loud she's bruising your gin. It doesn't matter if the building is on fire, the sky is falling, or the whole Goddamn Russian army is down in the lobby waiting for the elevator—there's no reason to scream that loud, especially not in response to Chase's clumsy fumblings. Time to cool her ardor.

It Worked for Poe

Using whatever tools you have and trusting her screams to cover the sound of your labor, seal the door to her apartment. It may be too much to ask that there be enough bricks and mortar just lying around to do a slap-up *Cask of Amontillado*, but if you have enough cement, caulk, or other fixative to smear around the edges of her door, it will muffle the echoes of her passion and keep Chase from sneaking out before she wakes up. They'll have an excellent opportunity to really get to know each other between her increasingly frantic calls to the super.

Outgun Her

During some period of the day when you're not at home but she is, rent out your apartment as practice space to opera students. It won't be terribly pleasant to have the students around your stuff, but the malicious joy you'll get from beating her at her own game may make it worth it. If she ends up seducing the opera singer, move.

Program Notes

Write up a measured critique of her performance in the same prim, condescending style used by *The New York Times*' theatre critics and slip it under her door. It may not shame her, but you'll finally get to use the phrase "clitoral histrionics" in a piece of writing.

There's a slim chance that she's making so much noise because Chase genuinely is the best lover of our generation. If you feel like it, stand in the hall wearing a low-cut blouse when he leaves next time and see if he asks you if you "need a Chaser."

Accept Christ and Sign This Petition: When Opinions Go Door-to-Door

There's something unsettling about any group that tries to recruit new members by going door-to-door. It's too aggressive, too reminiscent of the phrase "house-to-house fighting" and little cautionary tales beginning "First, they came for the Misanthropes . . ." The classic groups that work this way are religions, primarily Mormons and Jehovah's Witnesses, but they're far from the only ones. Any lunatic with an obsession and a legal pad can start a petition and become part of the solution instead of part of the problem, and they love accosting you in your own doorway and explaining why it's urgent—urgent!—that we take action *now*. Otherwise, the cumulative stress from moving the clocks forward for Daylight Saving Time will fry the grid, release the nukes, and blow us all to hell, so sign here and tell the President that we mean business about repealing DST, which originally stood for Dog Star Time, because aliens from the star Sirius got FDR elected . . . You see where this is going. The best and cleanest solution is to never answer the doorbell, but in case you're expecting the grades from your correspondence course and *have* to see who it is, here's how to keep from having to join up just so they'll go away.

Sexual Harassment as Panacea

"I'll join, sign, or endorse anything you put in front of me if you give me a hand job right here on the porch. I guess it's up to you. Do you really think this is important? Do you really need *every* signature you can *possibly* get?"

Easiest Sale of the Day

Enthusiastically sign up for anything they offer, using your arch-nemesis' contact information. It's a cheap shot and not particularly creative, but he can't effectively plot against you if he's running downstairs to answer the doorbell every fifteen minutes, can he?

Copyeditors Do It According to the *Chicago Manual of Style*

Take whatever literature they have and promise to return it with edits next week. Remember to check for mechanics and usage as well as content, always assign a grade, and try to leave helpful feedback—"Timmy. Your story is very creative, but has several plot holes and the characters don't always ring true. Keep working on it, and feel free to ask for my input on a future draft. Your work has potential, but you need to work on self-discipline and the editing process."

HOW YOU CAN PROVE THAT FDR WAS AN ALIEN:

Those little cigarillos he smoked weren't cigarillos, they were *transmitter beacons*. He knew he could call on the Sirius Star Armada to come in and help if it looked like the Axis was going to win, but he didn't want to do it too soon and tip his hand to Stalin.

Chapter 10

. . . AND GOOD RIDDANCE

{ The Death of a Misanthrope }

Well, here we are. The race is nearly run, the song is nearly sung, and the ice is rattling around at the bottom of your Collins glass. As the last few grains of sand dance their way to the bottom of the hourglass and the hospital chaplain leads the chorus of onlookers in a rendition of "How Deep Is Your Love?", this is no time to go soft. Be the first corpse the coroner has ever seen with rigor mortis holding both middle fingers in their full, upright, locked positions. Die as you lived and bank on a God who values consistency over chicken-shit last minute conversions. Nobody likes a quitter.

The Monkeys Get It All: Deciding What Happens to Your Estate

Considering the Misanthrope's natural reluctance to buy the whole bar a round or sign up for a package tour, many of us reach the end of life with a fair amount of cash on hand. Even after accounting for final expenses (in this case, a plot away from the crowd and a casket that locks from the inside), you may still find yourself with an estate to dispose of. In the all-too-likely event that you're not wild about your next-of-kin, here are a few ideas.

The Pharaoh Method

Whoever said "You can't take it with you" suffered from a serious lack of vision. If you can't pick someone to leave your worldly possessions to—don't. Sell everything, get it all in cash, and line your coffin with it. (Or swap the bills for gold bricks, if you want to leave the pallbearers with a hernia to remember you by.) Be warned: Centuries later, archaeologists may dig the whole shebang up and place you and your wealth in a museum, so be sure to include a note requesting a private display case.

Leave It All to Charity

Making a charity your primary beneficiary is a time-honored way of frustrating grasping heirs, but you can really salt the wound after you're gone if you give careful thought to just which needy cause gets the goods. For example: If your family has a secret Klan past, give it all to the United Negro College Fund. If there's not an obvious cause that will annoy them, pick the most obscure nonprofit Google has to offer. Being disinherited is bad enough, but being disinherited for the KwaZulu Leper Hospital will *really* sting.

The Karmic Hail Mary Pass

Many Misanthropes have deeply divided feelings about religion. While a single en suite in heaven is appealing, the general "love thy neighbor" concept tends to be problematic, if not downright impossible. You can try to regain some of the karmic brownie points you've foregone by leaving your fortune to a needy stranger. You could make discreet inquiries at a church or civic organization, but it will be easier and more fun to go through the phone book and choose someone with an amusing name. Tinkerbell Butterworth-

Sanchez will forever remember you as her anonymous guardian angel, which is the only kind of angel you're cut out to be.

POTENTIAL (ACTUAL) NONTRADITIONAL NONPROFITS:
Helping Hands: Helper Monkeys for the Disabled, Adopt a Donkey, Voluntary Human Extinction Movement, Dung Beetles for Africa, Brain Injury New Zealand's Zombie Walk

Famous Last Words: Choosing Your Dying Utterance

The most poignant line of a book is the last sentence. The most dramatic half of the play, the second act; the most melodious part of a song, the final note; and the most crucial part of the painting, the last brush stroke. It is what you say right before the end that justifies the beginning. So don't fuck it up.

Keep the Shovels after the Funeral

If you can time it right, this one's a doozy: "I've never told anyone this, but when I was young, I was involved in a bank heist. We took millions. The cash is gone, but there are seventy pounds of gold buried under the . . ." Gasp, flat line. If you underestimated the time you had left, you may need to paint a seriously vivid picture of the holdup. Describe the bank's luxuriously smooth Doric columns, holding the bank up with the erotic grace and power of an olive-skinned Grecian warrior raising his sword towards the heavens challenging Zeus to one final battle royale. Meanwhile, the chorus of your heirs screaming, "Under the *what?!* Under the *what?!*" like startled parrots will keep you amused as you wait.

Existential Despair

They knew you were difficult in this life; make them worry about the next one, too. Claiming visions of common understandings of heaven and hell leaves you open to ridicule: If you describe demons with swords, you'll hear a chorus of "What did you expect?" while if you speak of a soothing tunnel of white light, someone will undoubtedly say, "I guess they're letting anyone in now. Damn Vatican II!" Instead, tell them you see a Macaroni Grill in Gary, Indiana, located a convenient quarter-mile east of the I-84 off-ramp, and inside you see Harvey Milk, Michael Landon, Rod Roddy, Joan of Arc, and the guy who played Chief Wild Eagle on *F Troop* sitting down to a Romano's Sampler and having a round table discussion about the importance of fiscal responsibility.

"Smell Ya Later"

Why? Because that's just funny.

WHAT NOT TO DO:

Call each of your children to you in turn, cup their faces in one trembling hand and tell them how much you love them. And that it was not you who taught them, but they who taught *you*.

Undertaker Undertakings: What to Have Done with Your Remains

Misanthropes hate loose ends. The personality type that holds a bonfire of personal papers every two years "to cover the tracks" is not someone who ever says, "Oh, it'll take care of itself. There's enough to do in life without worrying!" As the Misanthrope nears death, he worries about a number of things: Is the afterlife just one big Rotary Club mixer? Will I embarrass myself by choosing to be surrounded by loved ones when the time comes instead of gracefully collapsing in a heap on the floor? And what will happen to my remains? If you've treated the funeral director like you've treated everyone else in your life, you run the risk of having your remains mailed to his ex-wife with a note reading, "Maybe here's a man who can stand you." While that would kind of rock, it should be your choice. Here are your best options.

Make It Irrelevant

Die in a way that ensures that your remains will never be found, like an explosion or a shipwreck. If you do it well enough, your heirs may have to wait several years to have you declared legally dead, which will be amusingly frustrating for them.

Have Yourself Stuffed

Eva Peron and Lenin both did it—not that they're the best of examples, but at least there's precedent. Cut a deal with a trusted local taxidermist to get "the works" after you die. See if it's possible to entail your will so that in order to inherit anything, your heirs must prominently display you in their home. "Oh, that's my uncle. At first I was annoyed at having to keep his preserved corpse in the living room, but now that we use him as a coat rack he's finally helping people."

Pass the Buck

Why on earth should you hold your heirs' hands through this one? You had to deal with this body the whole time you were in it.

Having to worry about what becomes of it after you're dead is like changing the oil in a car you sold six months ago.

Odd Things to Do with Your Ashes:

- Have them sold on the street as drugs
- Have them thrown on your archenemy, condemning him to an awkward trip to the dry cleaner and a visit to the eyewash station
- Have them fed to a pregnant dog, so that you might live anew through the puppies
- Have them placed in an urn with a small plaque reading that there are Spanish doubloons under your ashes for the person brave enough to reach in and fish around for them. There are, of course, no doubloons.

Going Around Again: A Misanthrope's Guide to Choosing a Reincarnation

Eastern religious traditions teach that the soul passes through many lives on its path to the convenience store for smokes enlightenment. Each life teaches the soul valuable lessons and allows it to work off bad karma it has accumulated through sinful or selfish deeds in a past life. Now, granted, the people who believe this are the same people who genuinely believe that chopsticks are a convenient way to eat, but there's still an off chance they're right about this one. The idea of going through life *over* and *over* and *over* again appalls the Misanthrope, since over time you might meet literally *millions* of people, and you'll have to go through puberty once or twice every century. Forewarned is forearmed: You may not have any say in the matter of where you end up, but keep these points in mind.

You Might Have to Be an Animal

In some schools of thought, a person may accumulate so much negative karma that he is reborn as a lower animal. This seems fun at first—when was the last time anyone said "don't worry, be happy!" to a cheetah?—but if the gods want you to learn sociability or are really into ironic punishments right now, they might send you back as a bee, ant, or other social insect. If this happens, go sting or bite a human being as soon as you can. You'll get to cause a little mischief; the human will splat you and send you into the next life right away. The gods will quickly discover you can take the "anthrope" out of a Misanthrope, but the "mis" is there to stay.

You Might Get Reborn in One of Those Crowded Countries

When Misanthropes are in the mood for a good scare, they don't bother with slasher movies or pulp paperbacks. They go right to the heart of terror and watch a travel documentary about Singapore. If you get reborn in one of those crammed-to-the-gills lands where the population easily exceeds the GDP, there's not a lot you can do except work hard, save your money, and retire to the Promised Land. For most people this means Jerusalem; for a Misanthrope it's Greenland.

Try to Cut a Deal

"Listen. If you send me back in a body that has awe-inspiring mystical powers, I'll use them to keep people away from me, *but* one Saturday every month I'll go to a high school, demonstrate my telekinesis, and then give a speech about how racism weakens us all."

ON THE OTHER HAND:

If you give a few dollars to juvenile diabetes research and pick up the occasional piece of litter, you may get to come back as a Mennonite. Then you can just screw a townie and be shunned forever.

Misanthropes Who Go Bump in the Night: Choosing Whom to Haunt

Well, that was unexpected. All the major belief systems were wrong; it turns out the thing that most closely predicted the actual afterlife experience was *Beetlejuice*. No dead relatives singing hymns, no black-eyed virgins, no pure and seamless oblivion: You're just a ghost. The novelty of walking through walls will soon wear thin, watching women bathe lost its erotic thrill when you discovered that ladies pee in the shower just like men do, and you were actually in the bank vault before you realized that you couldn't pick up the ingots—ghost fingers!—and that even if you could, there's not much a ghost really needs money for. It's time for a project: You're going to haunt someone. Here are some thoughts on choosing a target.

That Kid Who Tattled That You Were Hiding from the Presidential Fitness Test in the Boys' Locker Room in the Sixth Grade

I don't care if he grew up and spent fifty years vaccinating African children against river blindness.

A Goth Kid

There can't be much more annoying to a bona fide ghost than seeing a living, breathing sixteen-year-old dressed in red velvet, black lace, and white face powder talk about "the chill of the grave" and "the transience of flesh," then rub out a quick one to a blurry screen cap of Megan Fox's left breast before bounding downstairs to ask mom for a ride to lacrosse. A few blood-curdling encounters with someone who *actually* died should break him of that nasty habit of going to bed clutching a bouquet of dead roses.

Gary Busey

Is it all an act, or is he really that strange? Now you can know.

Madame Zuretzky

Find an up-and-coming medium who's convinced she can see beyond the veil. Show up once and get all kinds of poltergeisty, then leave and never come back. She'll spend the rest of her life trying to duplicate that success.

Your Best Friend

Just prank his balls off. Twenty years of pulling the chair away right as he's about to sit down *every single day* won't quite get you even for the time he tricked you into attending over-fifty speed dating, but it'll come close.

Beyond Bleeding Walls—Creative Haunting Tips for the Spectral Misanthrope:

- Hide all the fitted sheets
- Consistently move *Over the Top* to the number-one slot in their Netflix queue

- Turn their pets against them
- Emit a high, piercing shriek at the exact same time every day. They'll come to dread 7:45.
- Pill all their sweaters
- Have the faucets pour an assortment of fluids instead of just blood
- Produce a lingering odor of Noxzema

Candy-Stripers: The Final Insult

Except for the occasional tearful meltdown in a crowded Burlington Coat Factory, Misanthropes tend to carry themselves with dignity and gravitas. An upright carriage and frosty demeanor keeps Friendly Helpers at arm's length, and no one ever suspects that such a distinguished-looking man could have been the one to put a grass snake in the Salvation Army Santa's donation bucket. This history of poise makes end-of-life care especially burdensome for the Misanthrope. No one likes to be in the room when a fun-loving chronic-care nurse flings open the door, yanks up the blinds, and booms merrily, "And how are *we* today?" You've spent your life trying not to be included in anything more intimate than the census, and here this woman is including you in her pronouns. If you weren't already dying, it would kill you. The assorted nurses, technicians, volunteers, and candy-stripers come through the Misanthrope's room in their baby duckling-print scrubs and make a point to spend a little extra time with him, "since no one comes to visit, and he must so lonely." It's enough to make a man weep, but why not take more constructive action?

Die

This won't faze the nurses, but there's a good chance the volunteers and candy stripers have never actually been there for the final countdown. When you feel Charon beckon, hang on until MaKaela comes in to read to you from *Tuesdays with Morrie*, then take your final bow. The last thing you hear will be her startled squeak, and that's great exit music.

Rise to the Challenge

Cheerful hospital workers are so aggravating because nothing shocks them. Years of seeing the human body at its least functional have inured them to all kinds of horrors, and they've spent their careers toughening their mental calluses against patients whose time-weakened inhibition centers no longer recognize racial slurs as rude. They won't shock easily, but they haven't run into many Misanthropes. Draw on a lifetime of experience being unpleasant, and hammer away at them until their automatic "oh, you're such a kidder" is replaced by a muffled gasp. The last victories are always the sweetest.

Angels in America, Part III: Will You Please Shut Up, I'm Trying to Die and I Don't Want You to Learn a "Lesson" from It

People like this are always trying to learn life lessons and mine experiences for truths. Save the most receptive one some time with her dream journal and lay it on the line. "Listen. You live for a while and then you die. It's unpleasant, but tolerable as long as you don't have to spend your final days regretting never having gotten that bitchin' Hall and Oates back piece or having the nurse use your kidney cancer as a 'learning experience.'" If you deliver this in just the right tone of deathbed honesty, she may go get a Hall and Oates back piece, which is an excellent legacy for you to leave.

> The back piece features Daryl Hall and John Oates shirtless but wearing space helmets, riding jet-powered surfboards across Saturn's rings. It's pretty rad.

Going Out in Style: The Misanthrope's Funeral

Normals don't understand why a Misanthrope would spend his last days planning his funeral. "Oh, now, I don't think you should be *dwelling* on it," they say as they take the mortician's brochures out of your hand. "I think you should just trust us to handle it. Wouldn't you rather listen to this audiobook version of *Double Indemnity* instead? It's read by Jessica Walter, I know you like her." They don't understand that the Misanthrope's natural morbid bent combined with the certain knowledge that this is your last chance to make mischief means that planning one's own funeral is an even greater deathbed comfort than the morphine drip. Here are some options you may want to consider.

Broad Farce

Bribe your most mischievous little nephew to saw halfway through one of the legs of the bier. The goal is to have the bier still able to support the casket's weight, but barely. The first time someone brushes or leans against it, the whole shooting match will come tumbling down, and your corpse will flop out of the coffin and roll down the aisle. For the fourth time in your life, you'll have shocked an entire congregation into silence.

Assign Puny Pallbearers

Three old men, two teenage girls, and your cousin's son Bryce who does a lot of high school theatre. They won't refuse, since it's technically an honor, but the image of those twelve spindly arms slowly dragging your casket down the aisle, inch by inch, as the pianist reaches the end of "The Old Rugged Cross," pauses, and begins again from the top should sustain you during your final illness.

Mad Lib Eulogy

The mechanics behind this are extraordinarily complicated, but it's worth it: "Dearly <u>inebriated</u>, we are gathered here today to mourn the <u>fart</u> of Chris Turner-Neal. During his <u>69</u> years of life, he touched many <u>boobs</u>, as evidenced by the number of people attending this service today. He was fortunate to be able to indulge his love of travel, and visited many <u>rest stop men's rooms</u> during his time with us. His career as a <u>butt</u> brought him fame and fortune, and he is survived by his beloved <u>poop</u> and many friends and <u>turduckens</u>. He will be sorely missed."

If You Enjoyed Jessica Walter's Reading of *Double Indemnity*, Look for These Other Titles She's Recorded:

- *Faust*
- *What Color Is Your Parachute?*
- *Memoirs of a Geisha*
- *What to Expect When You're Expecting*
- *The Restaurant at the End of the Universe*
- *Divine Secrets of the Ya-Ya Sisterhood*
- *Love in the Time of Cholera*

- *Have You Heard About Radon? An Informative Recording for the Vision Impaired (Courtesy of the ADA Liaison Office of the Cuyahoga County Department of Health and Human Services)*

"He Was a Gilded God": The Misanthrope's Self-Penned Obituary

One of your authors once knew a woman who was widely regarded as the biggest bitch ever to terrorize Abilene, Texas. She swore, drank, stole, and gambled—she would have been a lot of fun had she not been so terrible. Her funeral was widely attended by people who wanted to be *absolutely* sure she was dead, one of whom passed a note to the organist requesting a quick chorus of "Ding, Dong, The Witch Is Dead." She was dead, all right, wrapped in her mink coat with a handle of vodka and a carton of cigarettes nestled in beside her in case the Egyptians were onto something and she was going to need supplies. The funeral was exactly what one would have expected, but the obituary was strange: It spoke of her grace and charm, and celebrated the kindness and gentle wit that made her sorely missed throughout the state. It wasn't until the last line, "She is survived by her beloved cairn terriers, Bluebonnet and Captain Jack," that everyone realized how such a full-bore baredtooth shrew wound up with such a touching tribute. She'd written it herself. It's a good idea for any Misanthrope.

Go Hard or Go Home

Newspapers have fact checkers, but they're usually busy with copyright law or the latest shit show in the Middle East. Don't be afraid to assign yourself a royal title and a few Olympic medals.

Bait and Switch

Write a tasteful, understated eulogy, and place it in a sealed envelope with your executor to be mailed to the newspaper upon your death. Neglect to mention that it is not your name that appears at the top of the obituary, but that of your arch-nemesis. If it slips past those same overworked fact checkers, you could create a mess that will take him years to undo.

Plagiarism

Use the plot of a well-known and beloved film as the template for your obituary. Those who read it will be strangely moved until they get to the part where you go to Mars and they suddenly recognize *Total Recall*.

Hire a Ghost Writer

Joyce Carol Oates isn't doing much lately, and she'd probably make you look good if you paid her well and compliment *Black Water*.

CONCLUSION

Take a deep breath. We know this moment is overwhelming—like losing your virginity the day you win on five consecutive scratch-off lottery tickets. You learned what a Misanthrope is, whether you are one or not, and if applicable what kind of Misanthrope you are, followed by a crash course in avoidance, deflection, and down-home, old-fashioned sociopathy. We've been where you are, but whereas when we found out we were Misanthropes we were armed only with Bartles, Jaymes, and a Dogbert mousepad, you have a whole book of helpful tips. You're welcome. And remember: Next time your office holds a luau-themed Christmas-in-July "morale-boosting event," you can slip out, take a long drag from your unfiltered Chesterfield, and gaze up at the sky, knowing that the same moon shines on at least two other Misanthropes, and in that moment we are somehow connected.

But don't call us. We'll be watching *Murder, She Wrote.*

ABOUT THE AUTHORS

Meghan Rowland, a group therapy dropout, was the only girl in kindergarten with a John Larroquette lunchbox. Chris Turner-Neal, an only child, is a graduate of James B. Bonham Middle School, where he received an F in participation. Together, they write the award-winning comedy blog 2birds1blog.com, widely hailed as "the thinking man's *Beavis and Butthead*" and recognized in NPR's 2010 Best of the Web. Sharing an author bio is an uncomfortably intimate experience for them both. Meghan lives in Washington, DC and Chris lives in New Orleans, Louisiana.

Meghan, exhibiting the "Don't Make Eye Contact" approach

Photo by Helena Johnson

Chris, in the "Deeply Contemplative, Don't Disturb Me" pose

Photo by Brandon Walker

Want Some More?

Hit up our humor blog, The Daily Bender, to get your fill of all things funny—be it subversive, odd, offbeat, or just plain mean. The Bender editors are there to get you through the day and on your way to happy hour. Whether we're linking to the latest video that made us laugh or calling out (or bullshit on) whatever's happening, we've got what you need for a good laugh.

If you like our book, you'll love our blog. (And if you hated it, "man up" and tell us why.) Visit The Daily Bender for a shot of humor that'll serve you until the bartender can.

Sign up for our newsletter at

www.adamsmedia.com/blog/humor

and download our Top Ten Maxims No Man Should Live Without.

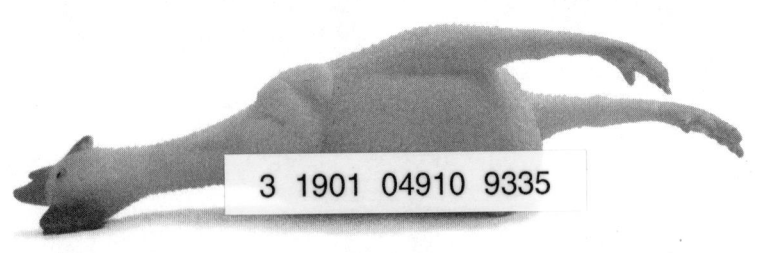